Tales of the Northwoods

Tales of the Northwoods

Echoes from Rhinelander's Past

By

Mark J. Miazga

Hodag Press®

Publication Data:

Miazga, Mark J. 1968-
Tales of the Northwoods: Echoes From Rhinelander's Past
Includes bibliographical references.

1. Rhinelander, Wisconsin—History
2. Baseball, Wisconsin, Rhinelander—History
3. Tramps, Wisconsin, Rhinelander—History
4. Brewing Companies, Wisconsin, Rhinelander—History
5. Dillinger, John 1903-1934
6. Criminals, Middle West—History
7. Basketball, Wisconsin, Rhinelander—History

I. Title

ISBN 0-9653745-2-1

Hodag Press®
131st Street West
Savage, MN 55378

This book is dedicated to my parents Henry Miazga and Laura Bixby Miazga who have taught me a love of family, learning, history, and writing.

Acknowledgements

This book started out as a group of stories that I always thought needed to be told to a broader audience. I am grateful for the help of Kurt Kortenhof who assisted me in countless ways in the development of this book. In particular, I am grateful for his editing assistance and research suggestions. I have become a more disciplined researcher and better writer as a result.

Special thanks are also due my family for sharing their knowledgeable and insightful memories of growing up in the northwoods of Rhinelander. Thanks also to Vicki Miazga and Kristin Larsen for editing the chapters as they developed. Kris Adams Wendt and the staff at the Rhinelander Public Library allowed me to view and copy some of the pictures in the library's collection. Kris also provided me with excellent information on the Rhinelander Brewery. June Thiel allowed me to research historical collections at the Rhinelander Historical Society. The Jack Cory collection was especially helpful. Eldore Huebner provided wonderful feedback for my chapter on the hobo jungle and the staff at Little Bohemia allowed me to tour the buildings and expand my knowledge of the shootout there. Thank you to my family for their unconditional support in all my endeavors. Finally, thank you to my wife Linda for her support during these last two years as this project developed and came to fruition. –MJM

Saint Paul, Minnesota
July 2002

Table of Contents

Chapter 1
John Dillinger, Little Bohemia and the Rhinelander Connections ... 8

Chapter 2
Presidential Ambitions and the Northwoods ... 27

Chapter 3
Early Popularity of Rhinelander Baseball ... 37

Chapter 4
John Kotz: Rhinelander Basketball Legend ... 59

Chapter 5
Rhinelander's Hobo Jungle ... 69

Chapter 6
Rhinelander Beer and the Rhinelander Brewery ... 81

Chapter One

John Dillinger, Little Bohemia and the Rhinelander Connections

Many local residents are aware of John Dillinger's famous 1934 shootout with FBI agents at Little Bohemia in Manitowish Waters. However, not as many residents are aware of the significance that Rhinelander played during that famous period in the history of northern Wisconsin.

To understand the emotion and excitement of the period, one must begin with an understanding of major news events during the year of 1934. 1934 was one of the worst years of the Great Depression for American citizens. Banks were having tremendous problems. Many of them failed, sweeping away the life savings of millions of hard-working people. Many banks that stayed in business foreclosed on people's homes, farms and businesses as the economy went from bad to worse. Because of the foreclosures and failings, banks were not very popular institutions in the eyes of most Americans. In fact, because of these foreclosures and failings and the fact that bank robbers during this time rarely took a human life, bank robberies and bank robbers avoided negative perceptions. The banks themselves were often considered more criminal than the people who robbed them. Bank robber Harry Pierpont captured this sentiment best. His self-serving rationale for robbing banks was that "I stole from the bankers who stole from the people." Charles "Pretty Boy Floyd" and other robbers even showed signs of charity by destroying mortgage records during their bank heists. A Depression-weary American public who did not yet know television, followed the activities of these bank robbers like a running television series. Daring daytime robberies and skillful getaways were glamorous and exciting, especially when so many Americans viewed the bank robbers as the good guys. Adding to this excitement was the unfortunate violence that sometimes accompanied these robberies. Law enforcement officials and regular citizens were occasionally killed during these robberies and getaways. At this point, fearful and confused Americans did not know which forces to trust in a growingly poor society. They were probably torn by the question of what forces were responsible for the substantial poverty of the Great Depression.[1]

Of all the Depression-era bank robbers and bandits who roamed the United States at this time – Machine Gun Kelly, Alvin Karpis, Pretty Boy Floyd, Ma Barker and her murderous sons, and Clyde Barrow and Bonnie Parker ("Bonnie and Clyde") – none angered FBI Director J. Edgar Hoover more than Indiana bank robber John Dillinger. When the vitriolic Hoover characterized these felons as "craven beasts," "vermin" and "scum from the boiling pot of the underworld," most Americans believed him. But it angered him incessantly to know that in Dillinger's case, much of the public was not buying his ire as Dillinger constantly avoided local and state police in getting away after his bank-robbing heists. Between May 1933 and January 1934, Dillinger and his gang pulled several bank robberies without being caught.[2]

They also plundered the police arsenals at Auburn, Indiana, and Peru, Indiana, stealing several machine guns, rifles, and revolvers, a quantity of ammunition, and several bulletproof vests. On December 14, 1933, John Hamilton, a Dillinger gang member, shot and killed a police detective in Chicago. A month later, a member of the Dillinger gang killed a police officer during the robbery of the First National Bank of East Chicago, Indiana. Then the gang made their way to Florida and, subsequently, to Tucson, Arizona. There on January 23, 1934, a fire broke out in the hotel where two of Dillinger's accomplices were staying. Firemen recognized the men and local police arrested them, as well as Dillinger. They also seized three Thompson submachine guns, two Winchester rifles, five bulletproof vests, and more than $25,000 in cash, part of which came from the East Chicago robbery.[3]

By now Dillinger's fame was spreading, Hoover's interest in apprehending him increasing, and Dillinger's greatest fame as well as his well-known visit to northern Wisconsin on the immediate horizon. After the arrest in Arizona, Dillinger and others were sequestered at the county jail in Crown Point, Indiana to await trial for the murder of the East Chicago police officer. Authorities boasted that the jail was "escape proof." But on March 3, 1934, Dillinger managed to escape.

On the morning of March 3rd, jail attendant Sam Cahoon unlocked Dillinger's cell door for the morning cleanup. Dillinger then stuck a gun to the attendant's stomach and ordered him into the cell. The "gun" is widely believed to have been a crudely carved piece of dark wood and not a real gun at all. Nonetheless, Dillinger had taken the attendant captive and ordered him to call the Deputy Sheriff into the cell. After trapping these two individuals, Dillinger had the Deputy Sheriff call the warden who also fell into the trap set by Dillinger. With machine guns taken from the warden's office, Dillinger and another prisoner, Herbert Youngblood, captured a dozen guards. They then gathered a couple of hostages into the sheriff's car and drove to the Illinois state line where they gave the hostages a few dollars and released them.[4]

When Dillinger drove the sheriff's car across the Illinois state line, he committed his first federal offense. At the time, bank robbery was a local matter, but violations of the National Motor Vehicle Theft Act came under the jurisdiction of the Federal Bureau of Investigation.[5] Now Hoover had his chance. The FBI immediately joined in the manhunt for John Dillinger. Hoover handed the Dillinger project over to Melvin Purvis, the head of the FBI's Chicago field office. While Purvis and the FBI set up traps designed to catch Dillinger, Dillinger managed to elude every one of them. While historical accounts differ slightly, it is generally believed that after Dillinger's March 3rd escape, he met up with his girlfriend Evelyn Frechette in Chicago. They likely proceeded to Saint Paul, Minnesota where Dillinger teamed up with gangsters Homer Van Meter, Lester "Baby Face Nelson" Gillis, Eddie Green, and Tommy Caroll, among others. Together, they robbed several banks including one in Sioux Falls, South Dakota and another in Mason City, Iowa.[6]

A couple of weeks later on March 30, 1934, Dillinger and his gang found themselves in a shootout with the FBI at the Lincoln Court Apartments in Saint Paul. Dillinger received a bullet wound in the shootout, but managed to escape another FBI trap. After being treated for his wound at a fellow gangster's apartment in Saint Paul, Dillinger headed back to Indiana.[7] By now he was the most wanted criminal in the United States. Dillinger stopped for a brief visit with his family in Indiana. On April 3rd, he and Homer Van Meter robbed a police station at Warsaw, Indiana of guns and bulletproof vests. From there, amid increased national news and FBI attention toward "Public Enemy Number One," Dillinger made his way toward northern Wisconsin.[8]

Shortly after Dillinger's arrival at the Little Bohemia resort in

Manitowish Waters north of Rhinelander, the FBI received a tip that John Dillinger and his gang were staying there. The tip came from a phone booth in Rhinelander. Mrs. Nan Wanatka, wife of Little Bohemia's owner and proprietor, Emil Wanatka had become nervous during the Dillinger gang's stay at Little Bohemia.[9] She told her brother in law, Henry Voss of her concern. Voss, who owned a resort only a mile and a half below Little Bohemia, suggested driving to Rhinelander to phone the FBI in Chicago for immediate help.[10] The next morning, after an hour and a half drive over bad roads, Voss made the phone call from Rhinelander.[11] After agent Melvin Purvis spoke with Voss, Purvis phoned FBI Director J. Edgar Hoover in Washington. Hoover told him to request the Saint Paul office to fly all available agents to Rhinelander. Assistant Director of the FBI Hugh Clegge, who had been sent to Saint Paul by Hoover after Dillinger shot his way out of the Lincoln Court Apartments, was still in Saint Paul and would head the entire Northern Wisconsin operation.[12] During the evening of April 22, 1934, four airplanes full of FBI and Department of Justice agents left Chicago and Saint Paul for Rhinelander. The agents stayed overnight in Rhinelander. Six men accompanied the Chicago plane, which landed at the Rhinelander airport shortly after daybreak. Arrival had been delayed slightly because the pilot spent a half-hour cruising, waiting for day to break so he could see the local airport. Rhinelander became the focal point for the FBI as they quickly gathered automobiles, armaments, and the assistance of local law enforcement officials. While in Rhinelander, the FBI kept their plans top secret. A temporary headquarters for the FBI was established while automobiles were being obtained for the surprise raid on Dillinger and his gang in Manitowish Waters. Local automobile owners rented automobiles to FBI agents for the surprise raid. They were not told the purpose of the trip. At first, they thought the federal men to be merely searching for stills. Rhinelander residents began to realize more than moonshine was at issue as FBI agents opened packages and suitcases in front of the local residents from whom they had rented the automobiles. To the amazement of the local residents, out came "tommy guns," bombs, tear gas, round after round of ammunition, rifles, shotguns, sidearms, bullet-proof vests, and other equipment. There was no doubt, from the display of weapons and firepower, that serious business was afoot, and that desperate gunmen were sought in northern Wisconsin. Residents still did not know exactly which gunmen were being sought. Several hours later however, word began to spread quickly around Rhinelander that one of the gunmen being sought was none other that John Dillinger, the most wanted man in the United States.[13]

Five cars left Rhinelander for Little Bohemia along difficult driving conditions. The road was muddy from melting snow and pocked with holes. After thirty miles, two dilapidated vehicles broke down and their eight occupants jumped on the running boards of the other three cars. It was now bitter cold and these men, encumbered by rifles and shotguns, had a difficult time hanging on. At some point during nightfall, the FBI and Department of Justice agents joined Melvin Purvis, the special agent in charge of the FBI's Chicago office, in a surprise raid on Little Bohemia.[15] In the dark, the agents accidentally fired on three innocent visitors to the resort, killing Eugene Boisneau, a visitor to the lodge who worked with the Civilian Conservation Corps.[16] The gunfire also wounded another innocent person in the FBI's mistaken belief that these individuals were members of the Dillinger gang.[17] Alerted by the gunfire, Dillinger and his gang slipped out of a second-story window and shot their way out of the trap. The shootout made national news. The headline on the front page of the *New York Times* on April 23, 1934, read "Dillinger is surrounded in a Forest in Wisconsin: National Guard Called." Later that week, the *Times* described Dillinger's escape as taking place in an April blizzard along impassable woods.[18] The shootout at Little Bohemia humiliated the FBI. Just before the raid, FBI Director J. Edgar Hoover had boasted to the national news media that his agents had Dillinger surrounded.[19] Frustration over the shootout reached the highest levels of national government. Senator Royal Copeland of New York berated the FBI for bungling the raid, suggesting creation of a rival crime fighting bureau made up of the best law enforcement officers from each state: "When Dillinger was hidden in the woods of Wisconsin, they brought up a lot of young lawyers from the Department of Justice and armed them and turned them loose. They should have called on local authorities in Wisconsin… They fumbled it again." On the morning of April 24th, Chairman Sumner of the House of Representatives Judiciary Committee in Washington, D.C. called his committee together to consider half a dozen bills aimed at better federal gangster-control. This was clearly in response to the FBI's failure to capture Dillinger at Little Bohemia the day before. Chairman Sumner proposed these bills in committee after a personal appeal from President Franklin Roosevelt. The April 24, 1934 *Rhinelander Daily News* reported that President Roosevelt's signal for congressional speed in bolstering the government's anti-crime campaign is clear and comes at a time of clear Roosevelt administration anger at Dillinger's latest escape.[20]

After the shootout at Little Bohemia, Dillinger and his gang escaped in three automobiles from the waterside of Little Bohemia. Dillinger, Homer Van Meter, and John Hamilton escaped to Mitchell's Resort, which was across the road and slightly north of Little Bohemia. As the Dillinger group was leaving Little Bohemia, Baby Face Nelson, who had been with them, went his own way. At Mitchell's Resort, Dillinger and his gang commandeered a car and had someone drive the car north through Hurley and eventually west to Minneapolis, Minnesota. Baby Face Nelson, meanwhile, intended to head to the Voss' Resort. When the FBI learned of Baby Face's location and confronted him at Koerner's Resort, Nelson shot at them and escaped. Nelson eventually ended up in Lac Du Flambeau where he stayed for several days with a Lac Du Flambeau tribesman named Catfish.[21]

Rhinelander's connections to the Dillinger shootout did not end with the establishment of the temporary FBI headquarters in Rhinelander preceding the raid. After the agents landed in Rhinelander, local resident Isidore Tuchalski agreed to drive Melvin Purvis into the business section of Rhinelander. On the way, Tuchalski boasted that his car was a "special job" capable of attaining speeds of 103 miles per hour. The FBI consulted Rhinelander's Ford automobile dealership concerning vehicles needed for the raid on Little Bohemia. When the FBI discovered it would take an hour to round up five autos for hire, they decided to borrow Tuchalski's Ford coupe and four other cars.[22]

Tuchalski's car was rented to FBI agents on Sunday afternoon, April 22, 1934. The car played a major role in the shootout at Little Bohemia and the immediate events following the confrontation. After Baby Face Nelson fled Little Bohemia, he ran to Koerner's Resort and demanded that the proprietor furnish him a car, presumably to drive to Voss' Resort or elsewhere. Before the proprietor could reply, the Tuchalski car carrying two FBI agents and a local constable pulled up outside. Shouting "Who's that?" Nelson ran out to face the men and opened a stream of bullets from his machine gun. The three men leapt from the automobile returning fire at Nelson. W. Carter Baum, a Chicago federal agent, was killed, Constable Carl Christensen of Spider Lake, Wisconsin received critical wounds, and J.C. Newman, a Department of Justice agent from Chicago, was grazed by a bullet. An injured Nelson managed to steal the Tuchalski car driving it several miles on a flat tire, ruining the tire and wrecking the wheel. It is believed that he then stopped, changed the tire and wheel, threw the damaged tire and wheel into the rear deck, put on mud chains, and proceeded. The car went only a short distance on the poor road on which Nelson was traveling. The muddy and seldom-used Boulder Junction road had been made impassable by spring thaws and it was here that Nelson abandoned the automobile and continued on foot.[23]

Tuchalski's car was found abandoned along the road and the car was returned to Tuchalski in Rhinelander by federal agents on the evening of April 25. The agents had removed the license plates so other officers, who were still seeking the Dillinger gang and Nelson, would not shoot at Tuchalski if they saw the license plate numbers. Police everywhere had been notified to shoot, and shoot to kill, if they saw a car bearing Wisconsin License No. 166-529. Federal agents kept the tire cover from Tuchalski's car, hoping to find fingerprints on it, to aid them in their search for agent Baum's murderer who, at that point, remained unknown. Tuchalski's bullet-pierced and damaged car attracted big crowds of spectators upon its return to Rhinelander.[24]

Yet another connection between the Dillinger shootout and the Rhinelander area exists in the possibility of a planned bank robbery in Rhinelander. Questions as to whether Dillinger planned a bank robbery in Rhinelander abounded after word of the Little Bohemia manhunt and accompanying shootouts spread through the northwoods. Much evidence substantiated this idea at the time. Officers who were in the law enforcement contingent at Little Bohemia heard reports that Dillinger had $40,000 in cash on him, and that he had made the remark that as soon as he pulled a bank job that would yield around $25,000, he would be ready to get out of this part of the state. It is believed that Ironwood and Rhinelander would have been likely target cities for the bank robbery, since Little Bohemia is about midway between the two cities and both cities had banks capable of yielding the payout Dillinger desired.

Rhinelander also may have been a more logical spot for the bank heist because it is on the way toward Neopit and Chicago and Ironwood is not. Dillinger's then current girlfriend with whom he stayed at Little Bohemia was a resident of Neopit in southern Wisconsin. She may have known the roads and area of southern Wisconsin well and better than either of them knew Michigan's Upper Peninsula. In addition, Dillinger had contacts and friends in Chicago and in his home state of Indiana that he may have intended to visit.

The April 23, 1934 *Rhinelander Daily News* reported that Dillinger and his gang arrived at Little Bohemia on Friday, April 21st and were spending time on trips to nearby cities. The intent of these trips is not known and whether they visited Rhinelander is also unknown. It is possible, however, given Dillinger's remarks, Rhinelander's larger banks, and a logical route leading from Rhinelander toward Chicago, that these trips may have been made to Rhinelander to plan a bank robbery.

Evidence of these trips possibly being made to Rhinelander is found in the report of Rhinelander police officer Arthur Johnson. Johnson's April 1934 report stated that Officer Johnson questioned two suspicious men during the week before the Little Bohemia shootout. Officer Johnson believed the men might have been "spotters" for a criminal ring. The men claimed to be from Chicago and staying at a Vilas County resort while looking for heavyweight boxing material. Emil Wanatka, the owner of Little Bohemia at that time, was a former Chicago boxer and boxing trainer. During the same week Officer Johnson questioned these men, Chief of Police Maurice Straub was called to an East Side tourist rental home. The landlord became suspicious of three men who rented a room for the night and appeared highly nervous. Before Chief Straub questioned them, the men left the house saying they were going to church, but instead jumped in a car and headed east on Highway 8.[25]

Although Dillinger and his gang had only been in the northwoods a short time, they created quite a stir in the Rhinelander area and across the nation. After the shootout at Little Bohemia, the Dillinger gang scattered in several directions. Dillinger, John Hamilton, and Homer Van Meter headed toward Minneapolis.[26] Baby Face Nelson ran his car off the road and proceeded on foot to Lac Du Flambeau.[27] After staying at the cabin of Ojibwa native Ole Catfish for approximately three days, Nelson walked toward Lac Du Flambeau. After finding a car parked near a lake, Nelson pulled out a gun an demanded the car keys from the owner of the car who was fishing nearby. By the next morning Nelson was 140 miles from Lac Du Flambeau when a connecting rod burned out in the stolen car. Posing as a Civilian Conservation Corps employee, he asked a farmer to drive him to Marshfield, Wisconsin. In Marshfield, Nelson purchased a 1929 Chevrolet automobile and left Marshfield.[28] He would later die on November 27, 1934 of gunshots received in a shootout near Barrington, Illinois.[29]

From Minneapolis-Saint Paul, the Dillinger gang began heading south. At a bridge over the Mississippi River just south of Saint Paul, the Dillinger gang escaped a shootout with local law enforcement officers stationed at the bridge.[30] Dillinger traveled to Chicago with Van Meter and Hamilton. Hamilton received gunshot wounds in the Mississippi River bridge shootout and died a few days later. Dillinger and Van Meter found a hideout in Calumet City outside of Chicago and they virtually disappeared.[31] Dillinger underwent plastic surgery to change his looks and had his fingerprints etched out by acid.[32] While in Chicago, Dillinger reinvented himself as "Jimmy Lawrence," a clerk at the Board of Trade.[33] He also moved into Anna Sage's north side apartment. Sage was someone that Dillinger trusted. Having operated brothels in Northern Indiana and Chicago, she was well acquainted with underworld figures who tried to stay away from the watchful eyes of law enforcement officials. Sage was also sought by immigration authorities that were trying to deport her to her native Romania.

Sage thought that helping get John Dillinger arrested would mean an end to her deportation troubles. While the FBI claimed they couldn't promise to stop the deportation, they did say they would do what they could to prevent it. Sage's part of the agreement with the FBI was to become an FBI operative. She teamed with Martin Zarkovich, an East Chicago detective, to arrange a plan for Dillinger's demise. Zarkovich wanted Dillinger killed on the spot. Chicago police angrily refused to have anything to do with an execution, but FBI agent Melvin Purvis, still embarrassed by the failed effort to catch Dillinger in northern Wisconsin, was receptive to this idea. Purvis, Zarkovich, and Sage conspired to have Dillinger gunned down. On Sunday evening, July 22, 1934, Sage phoned authorities to tip them off that she and Dillinger would be attending a movie that evening at either the Biograph or Marbro theaters. Dillinger went to the Biograph Theater at 2433 N. Lincoln Avenue in Chicago to see "Manhattan Melodrama," a gangster movie starring Clark Gable. Anna Sage and Dillinger's new girlfriend Polly Hamilton accompanied him. When the movie was over, the three left the theater and turned in the direction of Sage's apartment on Halsted Street.[34]

The official version of events states that Purvis then ordered Dillinger to halt. Surrounded by 20 agents, Dillinger pulled a pistol from his pants pocket and made a dash for the nearby alley. In a volley of federal gunfire, he was nearly dead when he hit the pavement. Many eyewitnesses recalled events differently. No one remembered Purvis or any other agent calling out a warning, nor did anyone in the crowded sidewalk see Dillinger pull a gun.[35] Thus, almost three months after his famous shootout in northern Wisconsin, John Dillinger's well-known career was over as he lay dead in a hail of gunfire on a Chicago street. For her part in apprehending Dillinger, Sage was paid $5000 from the FBI, but her request to stay deportation proceedings was denied. She would eventually die in Romania in 1947.[36]

Many older residents of the northwoods remember the excitement of this period when Dillinger was on the run. These events are yet another example of the colorful history of Rhinelander.

Courtesy of the Rhinelander Public Library

One of the automobiles used in the Dillinger shootout.

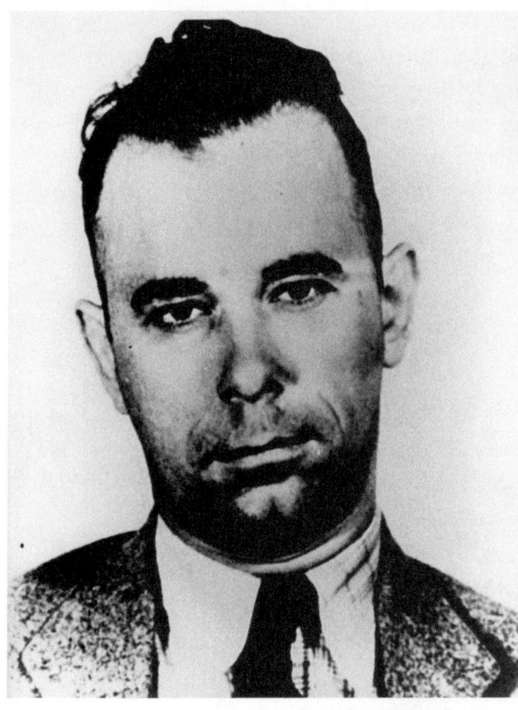

Author's collection

John Dillinger: Public Enemy Number One, 1934.

Author's collection

Former Federal Bureau of Investigation Director J. Edgar Hoover.

WANTED

JOHN HERBERT DILLINGER

On June 25, 1934, HOMER S. CUMMINGS, Attorney General of the United States, under the authority vested in him by an Act of Congress approved June 6, 1934, offered a reward of

$10,000.00

for the capture of John Herbert Dillinger or a reward of

$5,000.00

for information leading to the arrest of John Herbert Dillinger.

DESCRIPTION

Age, 32 years; Height, 5 feet 7-1/8 inches; Weight, 153 pounds; Build, medium; Hair, medium chestnut; Eyes, grey; Complexion, medium; Occupation, machinist; Marks and scars, 1/2 inch scar back left hand, scar middle upper lip, brown mole between eyebrows.

All claims to any of the aforesaid rewards and all questions and disputes that may arise as among claimants to the foregoing rewards shall be passed upon by the Attorney General and his decisions shall be final and conclusive. The right is reserved to divide and allocate portions of any of said rewards as between several claimants. No part of the aforesaid rewards shall be paid to any official or employee of the Department of Justice.

If you are in possession of any information concerning the whereabouts of John Herbert Dillinger, communicate immediately by telephone or telegraph collect to the nearest office of the Division of Investigation, United States Department of Justice, the local addresses of which are set forth on the reverse side of this notice.

JOHN EDGAR HOOVER, DIRECTOR,
DIVISION OF INVESTIGATION,
UNITED STATES DEPARTMENT OF JUSTICE,
WASHINGTON, D. C.

June 25, 1934

National Archives

John Herbert Dillinger Wanted Poster.

CHARACTER STUDIES OF MAN FOR WHOM STEEL BARS DO NOT A PRISON

The News-Sentinel

DILLINGER ESCAPES

Bitterness

JAIL

BANDITS HOLD UP BANK IN S. DAKOTA

Desperado Uses Gun To Overa

In Crown

Courtesy of Little Bohemia

Dillinger Headline from a 1930s era newspaper.

Author's Collection

The entrance to Little Bohemia. Manitowish Waters, WI, 2001.

Author's Collection

Bullet holes from the April 1934 shootout are still visible at Little Bohemia.

Author's Collection

Some of the Dillinger Gang's personal effects left after the shootout are on display at Little Bohemia.

Author's Collection

Author's Collection

The above two pictures are views of the area bordering the lake behind Little Bohemia where Dillinger likely made his escape.

Author's Collection

Voss' Resort was Baby Face Nelson's intended destination after the shootout at Little Bohemia.

Author's Collection

The author situated under a suit worn by John Dillinger. Little Bohemia, Manitowish Waters, Wisconsin.

Notes to Chapter One

1. For a better understanding of the plight of many Americans during the Great Depression see: Paul Maccabee, *John Dillinger Slept Here: A Crooks' Tour Of Crime and Corruption in Saint Paul, 1920-1936*, Minnesota Historical Society Press, Saint Paul, Minn., 1995; Robert Gough, *Farming The Cutover: A Social History Of Northern Wisconsin, 1900-1940*, University Press of Kansas, Lawrence, Kansas, 1997; Marilyn Bardsley and Allan May, *John Dillinger: Little Bohemia: The Crime Library: Feature Stories* website (as of June 24, 2002), www.crimelibrary.com/americana/dillinger/dillingermain.htm.

2. For Hoover's characterizations of Dillinger and his obsession with capturing him see Brian Downes, "The Dillinger Trail: Bank Robber, Killer, Folk Hero. John Dillinger Was All That And More. Sixty Years After His Death, The Curious Still Come To Visit The Landmarks In His Life," *Chicago Tribune*, 13 March 1994; Tom Hollatz, *Gangster Holidays: The Lore And Legends Of The Bad Guys*, North Star Press Of Saint Cloud, Inc., Saint Cloud, Minn., 1996, 37.

3. For a good overview of the Dillinger gang's myriad activities during 1933 and early 1934 see Downes, "The Dillinger Trail: Bank Robber, Killer, Folk Hero."; Rex Redifer, "The Dillinger Legend 60 Years Ago In Chicago, A Hail Of Police Bullets Ended A Hoosier Outlaw's Career," *Indianapolis Star*, 24 July 1994; Maccabee, *John Dillinger Slept Here*, 67, 116, 118, 206, 208-224, 299, 300; "Dillinger Escapes: Eludes Officers In Raid Near Mercer," *Rhinelander Daily News*, 23 April 1934. For a specific discussion of the Auburn and Peru Indiana bank heists see Redifer, "The Dillinger Legend 60 Years Ago In Chicago."

4. For a good discussion of the Crown Point events see Downes, "The Dillinger Trail: Bank Robber, Killer, Folk Hero"; Redifer, "The Dillinger Legend 60 Years Ago In Chicago"; "Dillinger Escapes: Eludes Officers In Raid Near Mercer." News accounts differ in the details of Dillinger's Crown Point escape, but it is generally believed that he escaped after an elderly jail attendant unlocked his cell door and Dillinger stuck the wooden "gun" in the attendant's side or stomach. One account in G. Russell Girardin and William J. Helmer's book *Dillinger: The Untold Story*, Indiana University Press, 1994, theorizes that a jail attendant passed the wooden pistol to Dillinger after resisting an earlier conspiracy that called for the use of a real weapon.

5. "The Dillinger Trail: Bank Robber, Killer, Folk Hero"; Hollatz, *Gangster Holidays*, 26.

6. Maccabee, *John Dillinger Slept Here*, 116; Hollatz, *Gangster Holidays*, 26.

7. Redifer, "The Dillinger Legend 60 Years Ago In Chicago, A Hail Of Police Bullets Ended A Hoosier Outlaw's Career"; Maccabee, *John Dillinger Slept*

Here, 218-21, 251, 299, 312.

8. Redifer, "The Dillinger Legend 60 Years Ago In Chicago, A Hail Of Police Bullets Ended A Hoosier Outlaw's Career,"; Hollatz, *Gangster Holidays*, 28; *John Dillinger: Famous Cases* on Federal Bureau of Investigation website (as of June 24, 2002), www.fbi.gov/libref/historic/famcases/dillinger/dillinger.htm, 3.

9. John Toland, *The Dillinger Days*, Da Capo Press, New York, New York, 1995, 263.

10. Toland, *The Dillinger Days*, 267.

11. Ibid. at 268.

12. Ibid. at 269.

13. For discussion of the FBI's activities in Rhinelander see "Federal Officers Came Here By Air," *Rhinelander Daily News*, 23 April 1934, 2; "Two Killed When Thugs Dodge Trap," *Rhinelander Daily News*, 23 April 1934, 1; "U.S. Official Gives Report: Raid Had To Be Made At Night Because Dillinger Planned To Move, Is Claim," *Rhinelander Daily News*, 23 April 1934, 1; "Agents Fail To Get Dillinger," *The New North*, 29 April 1934, 2; Gough, *Farming The Cutover: A Social History Of Northern Wisconsin, 1900-1940,* 151; John Toland, *The Dillinger Days*, 269-74.

14. Toland, *The Dillinger Days*, 273-74.

15. Downes, "The Dillinger Trail: Bank Robber, Killer, Folk Hero."

16. "Agents Fail To Get Dillinger," 2; Downes, "The Dillinger Trail: Bank Robber, Killer, Folk Hero".

17. Gough, *Farming The Cutover*, 151; Downes, "The Dillinger Trail"; Redifer, "The Dillinger Legend 60 Years Ago In Chicago."

18. Gough, *Farming The Cutover*, 150, 151.

19. Maccabee, *John Dillinger Slept Here*, 237.

20. For a discussion of Copeland, Sumner, and President Roosevelt's remarks see "Anti-Gangster Action Is Plea Of Roosevelt," *Rhinelander Daily News*, 24 April 1934; Maccabee, *John Dillinger Slept Here*, 237.

21. For a discussion of the Dillinger gang's escape from Little Bohemia see Joyce Laabs, "Dillinger's Escape Made Impression On Young Gehrke," *Lakeland Times*, 9 February 2001, 7; Hollatz, *Gangster Holidays*, 29-32, 34-37; Toland, *The Dillinger Days*, 278-82; "Push Manhunt For Dillinger," *Rhinelander Daily News*, 24 April 1934, 1; "Agents Fail To Get Dillinger", 1; "Dillinger Escapes: Eludes Officrs In Raid Near Mercer," 1. For a discussion of George "Baby Face" Nelson's escape from Little Bohemia and

accompanying stay in Lac Du Flambeau see "Think Nelson May Be Hiding Out in Northland," *Rhinelander Daily News*, 26 April 1934, 2; "Forced Indian To Shield Him Since Monday: Slayer Of Federal Agent May Be Hiding Near Squirrel Lake," *Rhinelander Daily News*, 27 April 1934, 1, 2; Laabs, "Dillinger's Escape Made Impression On Young Gehrke," 7; Gough, *Farming The Cutover*, 151, 155; Hollatz, *Gangster Holidays,* 31-33, 57, 59-65, 106; Toland, *The Dillinger Days*, 280-84, 289-91.

22. "Dillinger Escapes Mercer Resort Trap," *Rhinelander Daily News*, 23 April 1934, 2; Cory, "Dillinger Shootout Recalled," *Rhinelander Daily News*, 24 April, 1974.

23. "Think Nelson May be Hiding in Northland," *Rhinelander Daily News*, 23 April 1934, 2.

24. For a discussion of the episodes surrounding Tuchalski's car see "Think Nelson May Be Hiding in Northland: Tuchalski's Car, Which Agent Baum's Slayer used, Found On Muddy Road," *Rhinelander Daily News*, 26 April 1934, 2; "Federal Officers Came Here By Air," 2. For a discussion of Rhinelander automobiles being used by the FBI see Jack Cory, "Dillinger Shootout Recalled," *Rhinelander Daily News*, 24 April 1974; "Federal Officers Came Here By Air," 1, 2.

25. For discussion of the possibility of a bank robbery in Rhinelander see "Dillinger And Gang Planned Holdup Here? Think Mob Intended To Rob Local Or Ironwood Bank This Morning," *Rhinelander Daily News*, 23 April 1934, 1, 2.

26. Laabs, "Dillinger's Escape made Impression On Young Gehrke," 7.

27. Hollatz, *Gangster Holidays*, 62, "Think Nelson May Be Hiding In Northland: Tuchalski's Car, Which Agent Baum's Slayer Used, Found On Muddy Road," 2.

28. Toland, *The Dillinger Days*, 291.

29. Hollatz, *Gangster Holidays*, 64, 65.

30. Maccabee, *John Dillinger Slept Here*, 236-39.

31. Ibid at 236-43.

32. Redifer, "The Dillinger Legend 60 Years Ago In Chicago"; Downes, "The Dillinger Trail: Bank Robber, Killer, Folk Hero."

33. Downes, "The Dillinger Trail: Bank Robber, Killer, Folk Hero."

34. For a discussion of the events surrounding Anna Sage see Hollatz, *Gangster Holidays*, 39, 40; Downes, "The Dillinger Trail: Bank Robber, Killer, Folk Hero."; Toland, *The Dillinger Days*, 317-26.

35. For accounts of Dillinger's death outside the Biograph Theater see Downes, "The Dillinger Trail"; Hollatz, *Gangster Holidays*, 39-41; Toland, *The Dillinger Days*, 321-27.

36. Toland, *The Dillinger Days*, 340.

Chapter Two

Presidential Ambitions and the Northwoods

Presidential candidates frequently center their campaigns on urban areas and cities where there are many votes. Despite Rhinelander's smaller size, the city has seen a fair number of Presidential candidates and/or their families visit the area.

As early as 1912, Rhinelander's northwoods was catching the attention of the presidency, primarily through the efforts of Hodag creator Gene Shepard. In 1912, the *New York Herald* printed an article indicating that Shepard's Hodag was going to have pups.[1] Theodore Roosevelt had recently finished his terms as President of the United States at the time and was a noted nature lover, conservationist, and outdoorsman. Roosevelt was the driving force behind the establishment of the national parks system in the United States. According to Robert E. Gard's *This Is Wisconsin*, Roosevelt read the article and wrote a handwritten letter to Shepard in which he stated that Shepard was "nothin' but a damned nature faker, cause there ain't any such animal."[2] Sixteen years later, Northern Wisconsin again gained the attention of the presidency when, in June of 1928, President Calvin Coolidge arrived in Northern Wisconsin to fish the Brule River.[3]

Perhaps the most frequent visitor to the northwoods both during and after his presidency was President Dwight D. Eisenhower. Eisenhower visited northern Wisconsin during his presidential years of 1952-1960 and after.[4] Eisenhower made at least six trips to the region, primarily to the Minocqua-Woodruff area. His last trip found the president and his wife Mamie arriving at Woodruff on a special Pennsylvania car attached to a Northwestern train on July 20, 1965. They stayed at the Lake Minocqua home of Howard Young. The special car was held at Ashland until Sunday, August 1, when it was returned to Woodruff to take the Eisenhowers back to their Gettysburg,

Pennsylvania home. During his 13-day visit, he spent a great deal of time fishing. On the last Thursday he was in the area, he attended ceremonies at the Indian Bowl in Lac Du Flambeau. He was made an honorary chief of the Ojibwe nation and given the name Gi-No-Wi-Gig by Edward Mitchell and Alex Bobidosh of the tribal council.[5] Although no one was sure of the exact meaning of the name, tribal members thought it meant a big bird resembling an eagle which soared high in the sky and seldom rested. Between 3,200 and 3,500 people packed the Indian Bowl that evening for the ceremonies. Eisenhower was very pleased with the honorary title and name. After receiving tribal clothing, Eisenhower joked with tribal members telling them "Now that I'm a full fledged member of the Ojibwe tribe, and, I hope, one of its warriors, I think we ought to do something about these palefaces. The first thing I thought of doing was to drive them back to the Atlantic Ocean, but there are a lot of them. So, maybe we ought to adopt all of them into the tribe, then the Ojibwes can run the whole nation." After the ceremony was over, Eisenhower shook hands with each of the members of the Ojibwe dance party. The Ojibwes called the handshake "the friendship shake."[6] On Friday night, he attended the Min-Aqua-Bat water show at the Aqua Bowl in Minocqua. Eisenhower's party stayed for about an hour until the show was cut short by rain. During the intermission, he told the crowd that he had seen a water ski show a few years ago in Acapulco and "that show couldn't hold a candle to these kids."[7]

On Sunday morning, August 1, 1965, Eisenhower left Woodruff en route to Rhinelander. The Rhinelander visit had been partially arranged by Arvid (Ted) Johnson of McNaughton. Johnson was the owner and operator of the Rustic Lodge Deaf Camp near McNaughton. He had telephoned the Howard Young residence where the Eisenhowers were staying and inquired whether the President would meet with the deaf children. Several days had passed and then Johnson was informed that he and the children were to be at the Chicago and NorthWestern Railway train depot in Rhinelander on Sunday morning. The train pulled into the depot at approximately 11:45 A.M. that morning. Upon arrival, Eisenhower emerged from his private rail car, waved to the crowd of approximately 1,000 people, and then looked around for the children who he had wanted to give top priority to. The ten children and their counsellors stepped aboard the rear platform of his rail car and arranged themselves around him for pictures. Eisenhower also spoke with the children through the use of a sign language interpreter. After meeting with this group, Mrs. Eisenhower emerged beside her husband at the rear of the train. Both appeared to enjoy their warm Rhinelander reception and waved their greetings to the crowd long after the train started to roll out of the depot amid cheers of "Come back again, Ike."[8]

While Eisenhower's brief appearance in Rhinelander was memorable, it was John F. Kennedy and his family who made perhaps the most memorable visits to the Rhinelander area. The earliest visit by the Kennedy's was on September 26, 1959 when Senator John and Jackie Kennedy made a visit to Rhinelander.[9] At the time of their visit to Rhinelander, John Kennedy was a senator from Massachusetts with ambition to be President, although he had not yet announced his bid for the presidency. Kennedy's visit was likely made with the intention of building up local Democratic party and labor union support in anticipation of the Wisconsin presidential primary in April, 1960. Wisconsin was one of the first state Presidential primaries in the country. Winning the Wisconsin primary helped candidates gain early momentum in the race for their party's endorsement as well as gain national media attention. The Kennedy's and their party flew into Rhinelander-Oneida County airport in five small planes from Rice Lake.[10] About 100 people met the plane and John Kennedy walked along the airport fence to shake hands with well-wishers. The group then moved on to the newly constructed Oneida County Labor Temple where the Wonder Hotel catered a reception and a luncheon. Several hundred people attended the luncheon with the Kennedy's including Henry Berquist, chairperson of the Oneida County Democratic Party. Berquist had an 11-foot Hodag behind the head table, and told the senator he had spent two winters manufacturing the creature. "I always wondered what people did in northern Wisconsin during the winters – now I know," replied Kennedy. Berquist presented Senator Kennedy with a replica of the Hodag. Kennedy was very pleased with his Rhinelander souvenir and later wrote Berquist: "We found the Hodag to be a very provocative conversation piece, and are delighted to have so interesting a reminder of our visit to Rhinelander." After Kennedy's speech, four Rhinelander High School students were allowed to interview and photograph the Kennedy's. The students were James Zerrener, Linda Durkin, Karen Rinka, and Virginia Zoncki. Afterwards, Senator Kennedy gave a press conference for northwoods media to question John and Jackie. Many non-local members of the press were also in attendance to cover the visit. These included reporters from New York, Boston, Chicago, Washington, and Milwaukee. News of

Kennedy's speech and visit reached numerous newspapers, radio stations, and theater newsreels. Television was not yet in the majority of American households as it is today. Radio, newspapers, and theater news were the primary source of news at that time.[11]

Only seven months after Kennedy's visit to Rhinelander, Kennedy won the Wisconsin presidential primary in April of 1960. Kennedy carried 21 of the 31 precincts in Oneida county outpolling both Minnesota Senator Hubert H. Humphrey and Richard Nixon. That election saw 77.45 percent of registered voters in the city of Rhinelander vote.[12] John Kennedy's brother Ted made an appearance in Rhinelander shortly before the April 1960 Wisconsin primary. Ted visited on March 18, 1960. During his visit, he attended a reception at the Labor Temple and spoke with employees of the Rhinelander Paper Company during the afternoon shift change on Davenport Street.[13]

Senator Hubert H. Humphrey of Minnesota also visited Rhinelander during his 1960 presidential run. Humphrey came to Rhinelander on Sunday, March 13, 1960. He was then the chief democratic opponent of Senator John Kennedy. Humphrey, accompanied by his wife Muriel, spoke to a crowd of 300 people attending a tri-state convention of paper mill unions at the Oneida County Labor Temple.[14] Humphrey's speech focused on the need to increase basic research in the forestry field. He was then the guest of honor at a reception at the Fenlon Hotel where he spoke and signed campaign cards for some of the people in attendance.[15] Humphrey would later become Vice-President of the United States from 1964-1968 under President Lyndon Johnson.

After the tragic assassination of President Kennedy on November 22, 1963, Lyndon Johnson ascended to the presidency. During his tenure as President Lyndon Johnson did not visit Rhinelander or the northwoods, however First Lady Lady Bird Johnson did make it a point to attend the musical *Hodag: A New Musical Based on the Exploits of Gene Shepard, Wisconsin's Greatest Trickster* in September, 1967. Mrs. Johnson did not see the musical in Rhinelander, but rather in Spring Green, Wisconsin. Mrs. Johnson was in Spring Green as a part of her national beautification program. She was also interested in a country festival of arts and crafts taking place in Spring Green. The festival was a cooperative effort of the University of Wisconsin Extension, Robert Graves, and the Upland Art Council. One of the festivals chief productions that summer was the Hodag musical. The musical was produced by Dave Peterson of the Wisconsin Idea Theater and it had originally opened in Rhinelander on July 18, 1964.[16] By the time First Lady Johnson viewed the musical, it had already been seen by numerous Wisconsinites after having toured the state and also Europe during the fall of 1965 when the musical was performed for American GIs.[17]

Few presidential hopefuls or their families visited the northwoods after 1960 with the notable exception of the family of Jimmy Carter. Carter had been governor of Georgia and was now campaigning full-time for the presidency. On April 1, 1976, Carter's wife Rosalyn, his son Chip, and his daughter-in-law Caron campaigned in Rhinelander. Rosalyn flew into Rhinelander for press conferences and short appearances, leaving later in the day for Superior, Wisconsin. Chip and Caron spent most of the day in downtown Rhinelander talking with local citizens, handing out pamphlets, and speaking to local media before leaving for Antigo and Wausau.[18] Ironically, on that same day another more controversial 1976 presidential candidate was also in Rhinelander. Alabama Governor George Wallace arrived at the Rhinelander-Oneida County Airport for a press conference at noon that same day amid very tight security.[19] Wallace had been a national lightning rod for controversy in the 1960s and early 1970s. He was best known for his opposition to racial integration through statements such as "segregation now, segregation tomorrow and segregation forever."[20] In the spring of 1963, a federal court ordered the admission of black students to integrate the University of Alabama. Wallace vowed to block the students from entering the university and stood in front of the schoolhouse door on the day the students were to attend. During the mid-morning, Assistant Attorney General Nicholas Katzenbach, under orders from President Kennedy, arrived to enforce the federal court's order. Wallace, knowing this would be covered by nearly all of the national media, took the opportunity to take center stage to speak on his segregationist views. Shortly thereafter, out of sight of the media, Wallace stepped aside as President Kennedy federalized the Alabama National Guard who escorted the students into the university.[21] In 1968, Wallace had captured five Southern states while running as an Independent for President.[22] By 1972 Wallace had announced to the national press that he had always been a moderate and no longer believed in racial segregation despite his national following of people opposed to civil rights for blacks.[23] During his 1972 preisidential run, Wallace was shot by a man seeking to be famous and not motivated by any political feelings.[24] In 1976 he was running as a Democrat against Jimmy Carter for the party nomination. Other than his press conference in Rhinelander, Wallace greeted some city officials and several classes of school children during his time in Rhinelander although it is unclear from media coverage of his visit what the substance of his speeches were or his platform. While it is troubling to understand why so many locals sought out Wallace given his past record of supporting segregation, Wallace's presidential campaign was already losing steam. After losing the North Carolina primary to Carter two months after his Rhinelander visit, Wallace conceded defeat and dropped out of the presidential race.[25] Wallace returned to the governorship of Alabama in 1982 and appointed a record number of African Americans to leadership positions in government by the end of his term in 1986.[26]

After 1976, no well-known Presidential candidates visited the Rhinelander area other than Independent candidate John Anderson of Illinois. Anderson visited in 1980. His campaign enjoyed some notoriety, but did not catch on nationally. Anderson would go on to capture over six percent of the national vote.

Although the Rhinelander area has not seen a visit by a major Presidential candidate in over twenty years, it is always possible that this dynamic may change as Wisconsin continues to grow in influence as a swing-state that has the possibility of being won by either political party in any election year.

Jack Cory Collections, Rhinelander Historical Society

Former President Eisenhower at Indian Bowl Ceremonies, July 29, 1965—Lac Du Flambeau, WI.

Jack Cory Collections, Rhinelander Historical Society

Former President Eisenhower greets children on the rear platform of his private rail car, August 1, 1965—Rhinelander, WI.

National Archives

President John F. Kennedy

National Archives

President Jimmy Carter

Notes to Chapter Two

1. Robert E. Gard, *This Is Wisconsin*, Wisconsin House, Spring Green, Wisconsin, 1969, 201.

2. Gard, *This Is Wisconsin*, 201.

3. *The New North*, 14 June 1928, 1.

4. Jack Cory, *Jack Cory's Scrapbook*, Northern Historical Society, Lake Tomahawk, Wisconsin, 1985, 111; *Oneida County: 1882-1982*, 164.

5. Cory, *Jack Cory's Scrapbook*, 111; "Eisenhower No Longer Ike; Now Gi-No-Wi-Gig," *Rhinelander Daily News*, 30 July 1965, 1, 3.

6. "Eisenhower No Longer Ike; Now Gi-No-Wi-Gig," 1, 3.

7. Cory, *Jack Cory's Scrapbook*, 111; "Eisenhowers See Ski Show; Will Leave Sunday," *Rhinelander Daily News*, 31 July 1965.

8. Cory, *Jack Cory's Scrapbook*, 111; "Ike Given Warm Sendoff," *Rhinelander Daily News*, 2 August 1965, 1,2,3; "Ike Greets Deaf Children," *Rhinelander Daily News*, 2 August 1965, 1; "Acknowledges Applause," *Rhinelander Daily News*, 2 August 1965, 2.

9. Jack Cory, "John Kennedy Got Warm Welcome Here," *Rhinelander Daily News*, 5 May 1976, 1; also see Jack Cory's newspaper clipping collection at the Rhinelander Historical Society.

10. Cory, "John Kennedy Got Warm Welcome Here," 1.

11. Cory, "John Kennedy Got Warm Welcome Here," 11.

12. "County Voters Favored Kennedy By Good Margin," *Rhinelander Daily News*, 6 April 1960.

13. "Kennedy Relatives Here Tomorrow," "Here Friday: Ted Kennedy," *Rhinelander Daily News*, 17 March 1960.

14. "Humphrey Hits Scrimping On Forestry Research," "100 At Reception For Humphrey Here," "Union Delegates Here Humphrey, Gov. Nelson, Haselton Speak Here," *Rhinelander Daily News*, 14 March 1960, 1.

15. "Humphrey Hits Scrimping On Forestry Research," *Rhinelander Daily News*, 14 March 1960, 1; "He Was A Busy Man," *Rhinelander Daily News*, 15 March 1960.

16. Gard, *This Is Wisconsin*, 45; Kurt Daniel Kortenhof, *Long Live The Hodag: The Life and Legacy of Eugene Simeon Shepard: 1854-1923*, Hodag Press, Rhinelander, Wis., 1996, 134.

17. Kortenhof, *Long Live The Hodag*, 134; "'Hodag' Tells of Gene Shepard's Pranks In Area," *Rhinelander Daily News*, 3 August 1965.

18. "Carter Family Works Area," *Rhinelander Daily News*, 2 April 1976.

19. "Wallace in Rhinelander," *Rhinelander Daily News*, 1 April 1976.

20. Program Transcript, "George Wallace: Settin' the Woods on Fire," *The American Experience, 1.*

21. Program Transcript, "George Wallace: Settin' the Woods on Fire," *The American Experience*, 11, 12.

22. Program Transcript, Part Two, "George Wallace: Settin' the Woods on Fire," *The American Experience*, 7.

23. Program Transcript, Part Two, "George Wallace: Settin' the Woods on Fire," *The American Experience*, 9.

24. Program Transcript, Part Two, "George Wallace: Settin' the Woods on Fire," *The American Experience*, 13, 14.

25. Timeline of George Wallace's Life, 1973-1998, "George Wallace: Settin' the Woods on Fire," *The American Experience*, 1.

26. Program Transcript, Part Two, "George Wallace: Settin' the Woods on Fire," *The American Experience*, 19.

Chapter Three

Early Popularity of Rhinelander Baseball

Fastpitch baseball has been a favorite pastime for many Rhinelander residents for a long time. There has always been some interest and participation in baseball, but there was no greater interest and participation in local baseball than during the period from 1920-1933. Local fastpitch leagues peaked in popularity and success during the 1920s. During this time, Rhinelander fielded a semi-professional team that captured the state championship as well as numerous teams in a very active industrial league. The story of Rhinelander baseball during this era is best understood beginning in 1920.[1]

Up until 1920, local interest in baseball could be considered mild. Before that year the Rhinelander city baseball team had difficulty putting together a full team for competition against other Wisconsin city teams. Whatever or whoever provided the spark for local interest is uncertain, but it is clear that in 1920 Rhinelander staged a real come back and produced a city baseball team that gave worthy competition to any team in the state. For the first time in many years, the city team experienced no problems filling its' roster and anxious competition existed for starting roles on the team.[2]

While first names are not always known, the local team of 1920 included the following players:

- Pitcher: George Carroll
- Catcher: Marquardt
- 1st base, Mgr: Al O'Melia
- 2nd base: Miles
- Shortstop: Bonnie or Hallenbach
- 3rd base: Joe Peterson
- Outfield: Hoffman or John Sohr

- Outfield: Art Post
- Outfield: Swedberg

This team had a fairly successful season playing their home games at the fairgrounds where Twist Drill is located today. Their schedule included teams from Antigo, Merrill, Ashland, Bayfield, Tomahawk, Phelps, Laona, the local paper mill team, Watersmeet, Michigan, and Niagara, Michigan.

In addition, Rhinelander's industrial baseball league of 1920 featured hardball teams sponsored by the Rhinelander Paper Company, Rhinelander Refrigerator Company, Daniels, Builders' Supply, and others. These industrial league games were played on an improvised diamond across from the present-day Printpack complex. The residential district was quite close, so windows in the surrounding houses were rather expendable. Two of the more notable teams of that year were the Rhinelander Ripcos sponsored by the Rhinelander Paper Company and the Rhinelander Airtites sponsored by the Rhinelander Refrigerator Company.[3]

By 1921, the city team was more commonly known as the Rhinelander Green Sox. The Green Sox included some new faces as well as many returning players from the 1920 team at their old and new positions. Players, by position, on this team included:

- Pitcher: Hoffman, Laroy, George Carroll
- Catcher: White
- 1st base: Art Post, Blake
- 2nd base: Mcdonald, Miles
- 3rd base: Jago, Deakin
- Shortstop: Duford, Hallenbach
- Outfield: Marquardt, Al O'Melia, Johnson
- Outfield: Art Post, Lutter
- Outfield: John Sohr, Karst

Competition for positions became more intense in 1921. More and more players were switching positions as new players joined the team and existing players found other positions where they were better suited to play or sat on the bench.[4] The changing makeup of the Green Sox' starting lineup is shown in the following three box scores:

June 13, 1921

Rhinelander: 10 **Hurley: 0**

RHINELANDER	AB	R	H	PO	A	E
Sohr, cf	4	1	1	0	0	0
Hallenbach, ss	5	0	2	1	0	2
Post, 1b	6	0	1	8	0	0
Marquardt, rf	5	2	2	3	0	0
Deakin, 3b	2	2	0	0	0	1
Miles, 2b	4	2	3	0	3	0
Lutter, lf	4	2	1	2	0	0
White, c	5	1	4	12	0	0
Carroll, p	5	0	0	1	4	0

HURLEY	AB	R	H	PO	A	E
Clifford, cf	3	0	0	2	0	0
Whitman, ss	3	0	0	3	5	2
Leo Hunt, lf	4	0	1	0	0	0
Harrington, 2b	4	0	0	6	1	1
Swedberg, 1b-p	4	0	0	6	0	0
B. Secor, 3b	4	0	0	0	2	0
P. Secor, rf	3	0	0	1	0	0
Lloyd Hunt, c	3	0	0	7	1	1
Schwab, p	3	0	1	2	0	1

June 20, 1921

Rhinelander: 4 Hurley: 5

RHINELANDER	AB	R	H	PO	A	E
Sohr, cf	1	2	0	2	0	0
Hallenbach, ss	4	0	0	1	5	4
Blake, 1b	4	0	0	11	0	0
Marquardt, rf	4	0	0	0	0	2
Deakin, 3b	3	0	1	1	2	2
Miles, 2b	4	0	2	3	2	0
Post, lf	4	1	2	4	0	0
White, c	5	1	2	4	1	0
Carroll, p	1	0	1	0	0	0

HURLEY	AB	R	H	PO	A	E
Clifford, cf	5	0	0	1	1	0
Whitman, ss	4	1	0	1	2	1
Leo Hunt, 3b	4	1	1	0	2	1
Harrington, 2b	4	1	1	1	6	1
Neugent, rf	4	1	1	2	0	0
B. Secor, lf	4	1	0	3	1	0
Swedberg, 1b	4	0	1	14	0	0
Lloyd Hunt, c	4	0	1	5	1	0
Schwab, p	4	0	1	0	4	0

September 6, 1921

Rhinelander: 4 **Stevens Point: 7**

RHINELANDER	AB	R	H	PO	A	E
Karst, cf	3	1	0	2	0	0
Duford, ss	4	1	0	1	5	1
Blake, 1b	3	0	1	9	1	0
O'Melia, rf	3	0	1	9	1	0
Jago, 3b	3	0	1	2	0	0
McDonald, 2b	5	0	1	2	0	1
Post, lf	3	1	1	1	0	0
White, c	3	1	2	3	0	0
Hoffman, p	3	0	0	1	3	1

STEVENS POINT	AB	R	H	PO	A	E
Schultz, rf	4	1	0	2	1	0
McKeague, 1b	4	2	2	10	0	1
Groh, 2b	4	1	2	4	2	0
Simmon, lf	4	0	1	3	0	0
Mormoyle, p&3b	4	0	1	2	4	0
Snow, cf	4	0	0	1	0	0
Gustin, ss	4	0	0	0	3	0
Kujawa, c	4	1	1	4	0	0
Wloszinski, 3b & p	3	2	2	1	0	0

The beginning of the 1922 season saw the emergence of semi-professional baseball on the local scene as the Green Sox added several new players. The local team was now considered a semi-professional or semi-pro team according to accounts in the *New North* and *Rhinelander Daily News*.[5] Semi-pro baseball included a mix of minor-league and amateur town baseball.[6] Cities typically supported a team, paying the players a seasonal salary and/or a fee of five to twenty dollars per game.[7] The team would play other semi-pro teams in the county or state. Rhinelander enhanced its' reputation as such a team in 1922 by adding players who had played for semi-pro teams before. The addition of such players likely elevated the status of Rhinelander's team and allowed the players and the team to catch the attention of more advanced teams. The changes that started in 1922 for the Green Sox are best summed up in a May 3, 1922 *Rhinelander Daily News* article:

> Captain Post of the Rhinelander baseball team announces the following new members of the team who are either already here or whose arrival is expected today or tomorrow for their initial appearance in a Rhinelander uniform. These players have been playing with big league teams or with semi-professional organizations and are well known among fans as being able to deliver the goods in any and every emergency. They are:
>
> Chester Palm, big southpaw pitcher who last season gained enviable prominence with Chicago semi-pro teams.
>
> Harris, catcher, of Park Falls, whose record is among the best in Upper Wisconsin as a reliable back stop.
>
> Burwell, another big time player, who will cover the second sack for the locals.
>
> Matt Gardner, the fast shortstop with the Mosinee aggregation last season.
>
> Stackovak, who did excellent work last year with Stevens Point and Schofield, recognized as a dependable hitter and fast fielder.
>
> Ed Paul, noted as the hard-hitting Indian pitcher.
>
> Shadama, outfielder, heavy hitter and reliable catcher.
>
> These, with the well-known local players, including Post, Blake

> and Carroll, will make up a lineup that will set a mighty fast pace for Antigo's strong team in next Sunday's opener.[8]

Other additions to the 1922 Green Sox roster included Donaldson, Propper, Sorenson, Herbst, and Kuehn.[9]

These additions to the 1922 team started the nucleus of a strong 1923 Green Sox team. The 1923 Green Sox played numerous teams en route to a 37-9 record and the state semi-pro championship. The team's schedule that year consisted of games against Merrill, Wausau, Antigo, Eagle River, Tomahawk, Milwaukee, the Madison Blues, Fond du Lac, Menasha, Hurley, Ironwood, the Chicago Union Giants, and the House of David. The House of David was perhaps the most colorful team played by Rhinelander that season. The team, out of Benton Harbor, Michigan, ranked as one of the best semi-pro teams in the country that season. According to their religious teachings, all of the members of the team wore their hair well below their shoulders and most did not shave. The team was likely quite a site for local fans that attended the September 7, 1923 game at the fairgrounds.[10]

During 1923 and the era of the mid 1920s, the Green Sox played some of their most memorable games. Two of the most memorable were against the Cleveland Indians and the Kansas City Monarchs. Against the Indians in 1923, the Green Sox led until the ninth inning when a home run gave the Indians a come-from-behind victory. The Kansas City Monarchs, an African-American league team who featured the legendary pitcher Leroy "Satchel" Paige, also squared off against the Green Sox. Against the Monarchs, the Green Sox played well, but lost. Paige did not pitch the entire game. He spent the first six innings walking around the field talking to local fans eager to see him pitch. Paige entered the game late and threw nine pitches. All nine were strikes, which no one could get a bat on. He then exited the game seemingly as soon as he had entered it.[11] Rhinelander hosted the three-game state championship series in 1923. This series between Rhinelander and the Madison Blues provided more memorable games as numerous local fans were able to see their home team win the state semi-pro title.[12]

Pitcher Walter "Wally" Tauscher was a leader of the 1923 state championship team. Tauscher finished the season with a 16-3 record striking out 137 batters and walking only 21. Tauscher also proved a formidable force at the plate hitting 371 that season.[13] After leaving Rhinelander, Tauscher eventually played major league baseball. He pitched 17 games for the Pittsburgh Pirates in 1928 and six for the Washington Senators in 1931.[14] Tauscher also played for the AAA Minneapolis Millers club for nine seasons from 1933-1941. In 1934 and 1935 he led the club in victories with 21 and 18 respectively. The Millers captured the AAA American Association pennant in each of those seasons. In 1938, Tauscher played one season with Ted Williams during Williams' brief stay with the Millers en route to a Hall of Fame career with the Boston Red Sox. During Tauscher's nine-year career with the Millers he amassed a record of 133-78.[15] Tauscher played in an era when major league baseball had roughly one-third the number of teams that it has today. Had major league baseball had as many teams then as it does now, it is likely that Tauscher would have won 100 or 200 games at the major league level. Despite Tauscher's short stay in Rhinelander, he is remembered fondly. He built his home on the 500 block of Pelican Street, was an active bowler, and very friendly with most who encountered him.[16]

Other leading players of the 1923 team were Jack "Lefty" Finnerman, Farber, Born, and Blue. Finnerman, a pitcher, went 19-4 on the mound that season while hitting 267 at the plate. Farber, the second baseman, hit 378, Born, the shortstop, hit 357, and Blue, who played first base and second base, hit 319.[17] Managers of this 1923 team included Irvin Loveton and Matt Gardner, who evidently replaced Charlie Bellile,[18]

After the 1923 season, the Rhinelander Green Sox gradually began to be less of a semi-pro baseball team and more of a compendium of the best players from the industrial league. The 1923 Green Sox had gained so much attention that many of their players left for more promising careers with more advanced teams. The 1923 team was made up primarily of the following players:

- Pitcher: Wally Tauscher, Jack Finnerman
- Catcher: Fitzpatrick
- 1b: Blue
- 2b: Grogan, Farber
- ss: Born
- 3b: Potter
- lf: Nuhlicek
- cf: Grogan
- rf: Wally Tauscher, Jack Finnerman[19]

By 1924, Tauscher, Fitzpatrick, Blue, and Potter had all left the Green Sox. The '24 team lineup included:

- Pitcher: Jack Finnerman, Lindner
- Catcher: Ulrich
- 1b: Duford
- 2b: Farber
- ss: Brandt, Born
- 3b: Huber
- lf: Nuhlicek
- cf: Grogan
- rf: Born, Brandt[20]

Despite the Green Sox fielding a less competitive team in 1924, city baseball continued to have strong participation through the industrial league. The industrial league was a local amateur baseball league consisting of teams sponsored by local merchants. It had been in existence since at least 1920 when interest in local baseball began to increase. The Rhinelander Refrigerator Company Airtites were a leading team of that league. The Rhinelander Refrigerator Company built a complete clubhouse for its employees and players. The clubhouse was converted from a residence that stood on the property more than a block south of the present Printpack plant. The ball diamond was north of the clubhouse. The club kept soft drinks in a Rhinelander-made refrigerator, card tables and chairs, a phonograph, and what was claimed to be the first crystal radio set in Rhinelander, on which, if you were lucky, you could hear KDKA in Pittsburgh, WCCO in Minneapolis, or WLS in Chicago. Some of the players on this team included Red Carlson, Charles Blitch, Allen Wight, Lloyd Denman, Joe Hack, Ed Swenson, Fidelaus Shorey, Ed Morrison, Charles Snaith, Lloyd White, and manager Forest Riek.[21]

1925 and 1926 saw the increasing breakup of the 1923 Green Sox championship team and continued popularity of industrial league baseball in Rhinelander. By 1925 mainstays of the Green Sox team such as Grogan, Farber, and Nuhlicek had left the Green Sox presumably to join more advanced baseball organizations, seek better employment opportunities, or for personal reasons. By 1926, Finnerman and Born had left the Green Sox leaving few, if any, members of the

1923 team on the 1926 roster. Some new faces appearing on the 1925 and 1926 teams included pitchers Johnson, Zeiser, Howard, Seifert, and Purcell; catchers Fred Klevenow and Purcell; first basemen Cholnard and Roelke; second baseman Kresse; shortstop Tulip; and outfielders Groff, Munson, Conway, Weyers, Barrett, and Blanchard.[22]

In 1927, semi-professional baseball ended in Rhinelander. During that year, the city team became an amateur team solely consisting of the best players from the industrial league who competed against other amateur city teams in the region. The team name was changed to the Rhinelander Rhinos and Fred Klevenow managed them. The industrial league maintained its' popularity with at least four teams playing in 1927: the Papermakers, Newsies, Businessmen, and Airtites.[23]

By 1928, baseball truly lived up to its' nickname of being the national pastime in Rhinelander. The industrial league consisted of at least eight teams: the Newsies, Refrigerators, Airtites, Juniors, Wildcats, Utilities, CourtHouse, and National Guards. There was an industrial league game played almost every night in Rhinelander and the Rhinelander Rhino city team continued to represent Rhinelander in regional play, playing at least once a week in the Wisconsin Valley baseball league.[24] Some of the players from the industrial league during this period are listed in the following two unique box scores:

June 15, 1927

Papermakers: 9 Businessmen: 3

PAPERMAKERS	R	H	E
Carr, 1b	1	0	0
Peterson, cf	2	0	0
Carroll, 3b	2	2	1
Richardson, lf	2	4	0
Mulray, ss	1	1	0
Roberts, p	0	2	1
Bolner, 2b	1	0	0
Johnson, c	0	1	1
Ammonett, rf	0	2	0

BUSINESSMEN	R	H	E
Novak, 1b	0	1	0
Keller, 1b	0	0	0
Christensen, cf	0	0	0
Plyer, 3b	0	0	0
Kuhl, of	1	1	0
Brann, ss	1	2	0
C. Finn, p	0	0	0
Anderson, 2b	0	1	0
Schellenger, c	0	0	1
Taylor, rf	1	0	1

June 17, 1927

Newsies: 13 **Airtites: 8**

NEWSIES	R	H	E
N. Davis, 3b	3	1	2
Lennon, c, cf	2	2	0
Swedberg, 2b	2	1	1
Kelley, 1b	2	3	0
Teake, lf	0	3	0
Vlahakis, ss	1	1	2
Schellenger, cf, c	1	0	1
Remo, rf	2	2	1
Olson, p	2	2	1
Johnson, c	0	0	0
T. Davis, cf	0	0	0

AIRTITES	R	H	E
Payette, 2b	1	1	0
Holszchuh, 3b	1	0	0
Swenson, ss	0	0	1
Shorey, 1b	1	2	0
Dobson, p, lf	0	2	1
Morrison, c	2	0	0
Lindwall, rf, p	1	0	1
Gravatier, cf	1	0	0
Ruggles, cf	1	2	0

Industrial league baseball likely continued to be popular into 1929, however, local newspaper coverage of it dropped sharply in that year. A highlight of the 1929 city team season was a visit from a Clearwater Lake, Michigan team to play the Rhinos. The Clearwater Lake team consisted entirely of Catholic priests. This team's success was well-known and proven by its' defeats of a long list of the best baseball teams in Northern Wisconsin and the Upper Peninsula of Michigan. Several members of this team had been offered contracts in organized baseball, but turned down these opportunities to continue in the priesthood.[25]

By 1930, the city team was known as the Rhinelander Ripco Ripples. The Ripcos played in the Wisconsin Valley baseball League while also playing teams from the industrial league. Players on this Ripco squad included pitchers Hurlbutt and Manley, catcher Fortier, first baseman Seidel, second baseman Peterson, third baseman Carroll, outfielders Maloney, Kuhl, Black, Tanner, and Gaber, and shortstops Felch and Riley. Floyd Creek was the team's manager.[26]

In 1933, the Rhinelander Ripco Ripples were eliminated from the Wisconsin Valley baseball league. The Ripcos were eliminated because of poor roads at the time in Oneida County and the long distance teams had to drive to reach Rhinelander from other Valley cities. After Rhinelander's elimination, a meeting was called by officials of the newly formed Northern Lakes Baseball League who were considering reorganizing the circuit in an effort to make room for the Ripcos. Cities expected to make up the new league included Antigo, Deerbrook, Crandon, Tomahawk, Eagle River, Phillips, Minocqua, and Rhinelander.[27] It is unclear whether this new league ever started up or stayed in existence. A new league that did appear in 1933 was known as the Hodag League. This league was composed of eight Oneida County teams: McNaughton, Lake Tomahawk, Crescent, Pelican Lake, Starks, Rhinelander West Side, Rhinelander North Side, and Monico. The Hodag League disbanded during the years of World War II. After the war, the league was again in action and remained competitive through 1950.[28]

The Ripco Ripples elimination from the Wisconsin Valley Baseball League was short-lived as they were again playing in the league in 1934 and continued playing until the years of World War II. After World War II, the Ripples continued playing in the Wisconsin Valley league along with a new Rhinelander addition, the Rhinelander Shorties sponsored by the Rhinelander Brewing Company. One annual baseball game local citizens looked forward to during the post-war years ws the labor day game. For several years the Hodag League all-star team played the Rhinelander Shorties in some very competitive games. Another popular game attended by locals was the Sunday afternoon game played at the fairgrounds where the industrial park is located today. The Sunday afternoon game was played by the Rhinelander Ripco Ripples in the 1930s and 1940s. These games regularly drew about 2,000 fans. Most of the fans walked one to two miles to the baseball park at the fairgrounds. The Ripples also played exhibition games against the Chicago White Sox major league team which also sparked a great deal of local interest.[29]

Post-war participation in local baseball leagues remained strong into the early 1950s and diminished thereafter due mainly to players raising families, a stronger economy providing more entertainment options for local citizens, and the popularity of the automobile allowing people to participate in activities outside the immediate city of Rhinelander.

Courtesy of the Rhinelander Public Library

An early Rhinelander baseball club, 1910.

Courtesy of the Rhinelander Public Library

The Oneida County Fair Grounds saw a great deal of baseball action in the first half of the twentieth century.

Courtesy of the Rhinelander Public Library

Rhinelander Refrigerator Co. plant and clubhouse which hosted many industrial league games.

National Baseball Library, Cooperstown, NY

Legendary pitcher Leroy "Satchel" Paige.

Author's collection

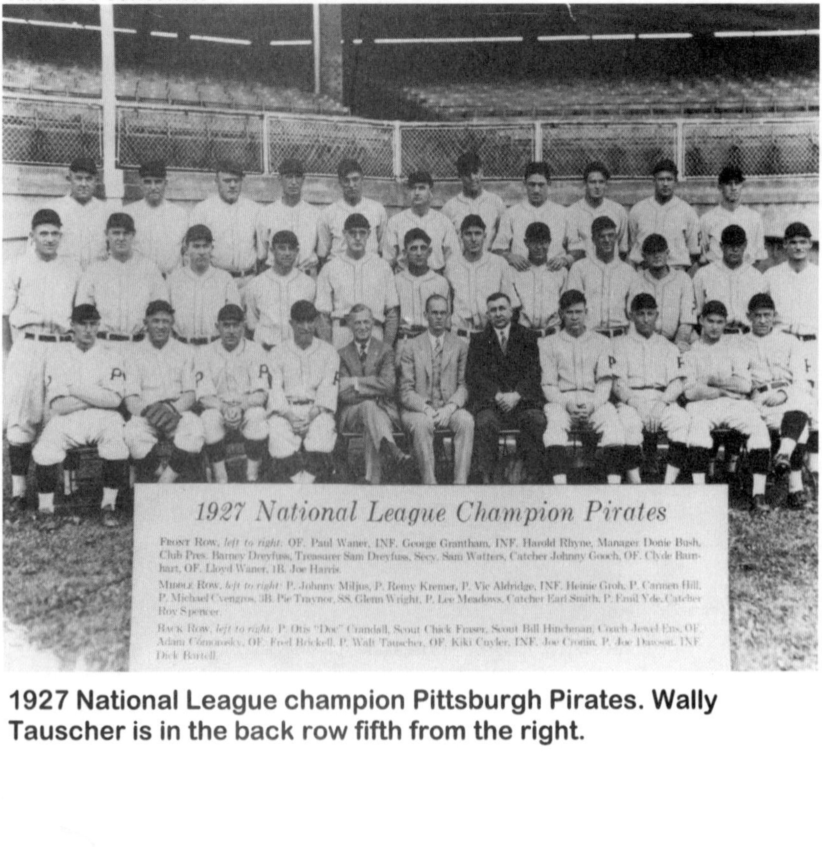

1927 National League Champion Pirates

FRONT ROW, *left to right:* OF. Paul Waner, INF. George Grantham, INF. Harold Rhyne, Manager Donie Bush, Club Pres. Barney Dreyfuss, Treasurer Sam Dreyfuss, Secy. Sam Watters, Catcher Johnny Gooch, OF. Clyde Barnhart, OF. Lloyd Waner, 1B. Joe Harris.

MIDDLE ROW, *left to right:* P. Johnny Miljus, P. Remy Kremer, P. Vic Aldridge, INF. Heinie Groh, P. Carmen Hill, P. Michael Cvengros, 3B. Pie Traynor, SS. Glenn Wright, P. Lee Meadows, Catcher Earl Smith, P. Emil Yde, Catcher Roy Spencer.

BACK ROW, *left to right:* P. Otis "Doc" Crandall, Scout Chick Fraser, Scout Bill Hinchman, Coach Jewel Ens, OF. Adam Comorosky, OF. Fred Brickell, P. Walt Tauscher, OF. Kiki Cuyler, INF. Joe Cronin, P. Joe Dawson, INF. Dick Bartell.

1927 National League champion Pittsburgh Pirates. Wally Tauscher is in the back row fifth from the right.

Courtesy of the Minnesota Historical Society

1935 Minneapolis Millers. Wally Tauscher is in middle of the back row, fourth from the right.

Courtesy of the Minnesota Historical Society

1938 Minneapolis Millers. Ted Williams is in the back row, third from left; Wally Tauscher is in the back row, fourth from left.

Author's collection

1927 House of David junior Baseball team.

Notes to Chapter Three

1. For an understanding of the popularity of baseball in Rhinelander see baseball coverage in the local newspapers during that era such as "Local Ball Team Wins First Game At Fair Grounds: City Team Defeats Papermakers By Score Of 9 to 4 – One Home Run Swat," *The New North*, 21 June 1920; "Ball Team Meets Phelps At Fair Grounds Sunday: Tomahawk Cancelled – Locals Strengthened By Return Of Old Vets," *The New North*, 17 July 1920; "Local Team Wins At Hatchet City," *The New North*, 12 August 1920; "Rhinelander Drops 2 Games," *Rhinelander Daily News*, 6 September 1921; Lloyd Cain, "City Team Wins Two Fast Games," *The New North*, June 1922 (exact date unknown); Lloyd Cain, "Three Out Of Four To Credit Local Team: Series With Rockford Maroons Results In Defeat of Visitors In All But Last Game," *Rhinelander Daily News*, 5 July 1922, 1; "Merrill Loses To Green Sox," *The New North*, June 1923; "Green Sox Win Two More Games," *The New North*, August 1923; "House Of David Baseball Team In Rhinelander Sunday, September 7th," *The New North*, August 1923; "Tauscher And Fitzpatrick Still Going: Are Brightest Stars In Game At Oglesby And Pilot Winning Team To Victory," *Rhinelander Daily News*, 27 September 1923; "Green Sox Now Semi-Pro Champs," *The New North*, September 1923; "Independent Baseball Champions Of Wisconsin," *The New North*, 20 September 1923, 1 (includes player statistics for 1923 Green Sox team); "Rhinelander's Wisconsin Semi-Pro Champions," *Rhinelander Daily News*, 28 September 1923; "Huber Stars As Green Sox Win 8 To 0: Lindner Invincible And Locals Hit Ball Hard Walking Away With Game 8 To 0," *Rhinelander Daily News*, 18 June 1924; "Three Stiff Contests Are On Schedule: Tomahawk Plays Here Saturday With Mosinee Here On Sunday," *Rhinelander Daily News*, 10 June 1925; "Finnerman To Get Try-Out With Brewers: Southpaw Twirler Playing His Third Season With Rhinelander Club," *Rhinelander Daily News*, 16 June 1925; "Poor Umpiring Mars Saturday Diamond Tilt: Rhinos Drop First Game 8 To 3, Take Second In 16-8 Slugfest," *Rhinelander Daily News*, 17 August 1925; "Lefty Taylor Allows Three Hits In Game: Ripcos Unable To Score Until Fourth, But Finally Win 4 to 3, Airtites And Independents Battle Today," *Rhinelander Daily News*, 5 August 1927; "Rhinos Upset County Rivals In Return Go: Lefty Taylor And Mates Hold Hazelhurst Without A Run Until Eighth," *Rhinelander Daily News*, 4 June 1928; "Newsies Play Guardsmen In Opening Game: Airtites To Play Refrigerators On Tuesday Night, Utilities In League," *Rhinelander Daily News*, 23 June 1928; "Priests Will Scrap Rhinos: Clearwater Lake Team To Battle Local Nine On Fair Grounds Sunday," *Rhinelander Daily News*, 27 July 1929; "Rhinos Spill Robbins Team: Northsiders Nose Out Invading Sugar Camp White Sox, 9 To 8," *Rhinelander Daily News*, 5 August 1929; "Ripcos Defeat Refrigerator Squad, 12 To 2: Collect 14 Bingles To Win As Hurlbutt Allows But Seven Hits," *Rhinelander Daily News*, 8 September 1930;.

2. "Tomahawk Will Play Locals At Fair Grounds: Hatchet City Nine Coming To Rhinelander For Game With Pill Wallopers," *Rhinelander Daily News*, 14 July 1920.

3. For discussion of the 1920 city team and industrial league teams see "Local Team Wins At Hatchet City"; "Ball Team Meets Phelps At Fair Grounds Sunday,"; "Tomahawk Will Play Locals At Fair Grounds: Hatchet City Nine Coming To Rhinelander For Game With Pill Wallopers"; "Local Ball Team Wins First Game At Fair Grounds: City Team Defeats Paper Makers By Score Of 9 To 4 – One Home Run Swat"; Joe Bloom, "Baseball Had A Colorful History In Rhinelander," *Our Town*, 4 July 1982.

4. For discussion of the 1921 city team, player names and the emergence of the name Green Sox see Bloom, "Baseball Had A Colorful History In Rhinelander,"; *Rhinelander Daily News*, 13 June 1921; *Rhinelander Daily News*, 20 June 1921; "Rhinelander Drops Two Games: Local Team Suffers Defeat At Stevens Point And Wausau Sunday And Monday," *Rhinelander Daily News*, 6 September 1921, 1.

5. *The New North* May 1923; "Season Opens At Ball Park Sat. May 12," *Rhinelander Daily News*, 4 May 1923.

6. Bruce Chadwick, *Baseball's Hometown Teams: The Story Of The Minor Leagues*, Abbeville Press Publishers, New York, London, And Paris, 1994, 45.

7. Ibid. at 44, 45.

8. "Heavy Hitters Are Here For Sunday's Game: Players Are Working Every Afternoon When Weather Permits," *Rhinelander Daily News*, 3 May 1922, 1.

9. "Baseball Year To Open Sunday," *The New North*, 4 May 1922, 1; *The New North*, June 1922.

10. For discussion of The House Of David Baseball team see "House Of David Baseball Team In Rhinelander Sunday, September 7th,"; Chadwick, *Baseball's Hometown Teams: The Story Of The Minor Leagues*, 44, 46.

11. For discussion of the games against the Cleveland Indians and Kansas City Monarchs see Bloom, "Baseball Had Colorful History In Rhinelander." For a brief discussion of Satchel Paige and The Kansas City Monarchs see Chadwick, *Baseball's Hometown Teams*, 46. (Chadwick also notes here that some major league players such as Babe Ruth and Loug Gehrig played either regularly or as "ringers" for semi-pro teams that would meet their price. A young Dwight D. Eisenhower also played semipro ball under an assumed name in the summer of 1910, Chadwick, *Baseball's Hometown Teams*, 45).

12. Jack Cory, "50 Years Ago Rhinelander Won State Baseball Title," *Rhinelander Daily News*, September 1974.

13. "Independent Baseball Champions Of Wisconsin," 1.

14. "Obituaries: Walter Edward Tauscher," *Orlando Sentinel*, 28 November 1992.

15. For an excellent discussion of Tauscher's accomplishments with the Minneapolis Millers see Stew Thornley, *On To Nicollet: The Glory And Fame Of The Minneapolis Millers*, Nodin Press, Minneapolis, Minn., 2000, 41, 43, 80.

16. Henry L. Miazga, interview by author, Rhinelander, Wis., 16 June 2001; Stanley Miazga, interview by author, Rhinelander, Wis., August 2001.

17. "Independent Baseball Champions Of Wisconsin," *New North*, 20 September 1923.

18. "Tomahawk Loses To Rhinelander," *New North*, June 1923; Lloyd Cain, "Antigo Victor In First Game," *The New North*, May 1922; Bloom, "Baseball Had A Colorful History In Rhinelander"; "Tomahawk Loses To Rhinelander"; Bloom, "Baseball Had A Colorful History In Rhinelander."

19.. "Independent Baseball Champions Of Wisconsin," *Rhinelander Daily News* 20 September 1923.

20. "Green Sox Open 1924 Season," *Rhinelander Daily News*, 17 May 1924, 1; "Huber Stars As Green Sox Win 8 To 0"; "Ally Wins For Sox With Paper Makers Sunday," *Rhinelander Daily News*, 14 July 1924.

21. *Our Town*, 29 May 1977.

22. For a discussion of the 1925 and 1926 teams see "Shiver Way through Cold For Win No. 2: Three Runs In Eighth Put Game On Ice For Bellile's Wreckers," *Rhinelander Daily News*, 11 May 1925; "Trim Mosinee And Tomahawk Over Weekend: Finnerman Holds Hatchet City To One Hit In Saturday Diamond Battle," *Rhinelander Daily News*, 15 June 1925; "Error Gives Victory To Bellilemen," *Rhinelander Daily News*, 20 July 1925; "Wilson's Poke Brings Defeat To Green Sox," *Rhinelander Daily News*, 22 June 1925; "Poor Umpiring Mars Saturday Diamond Tilt"; "Rhinos Clout Eight Homers: Purcell Hits Three, Huber, Mudloff Two," *Rhinelander Daily News*, 1 June 1926; "Blanchard Is Leader With .368 Record: Lebeau Has Perfect Fielding Record," *Rhinelander Daily News*, 28 September 1926.

23. For a discussion of the end of semi-professional baseball in Rhinelander in 1927 and happenings in the Industrial League see "Rhinos Clash With Crandon In First Game: Amateur Nine, Under Klevenow's Direction, Open Season Next Sunday," *Rhinielander Daily News*, 23 June 1927; "Wildcats Get Only Five Hits From Roberts: Richardson Big Gun At Bat, Gets Four Hits For Perfect Day," *Rhinelander Daily News*, 15 June 1927; "Leaders Lose By 13-8 Score: Squads In Tie: Each Team Has Been Defeated Once, Printers Garner 14 Hits," *Rhinelander Daily News*, 17 June 1927; "Airtites And Independents Battle

Today: Both Teams Expected To Use Patched Lineups, With New Bateries," *Rhinelander Daily News*, 5 August 1927.

24. For a discussion of the 1928 Rhinelander Rhino city team and the 1928 Industrial League see "Newsies Play Guardsmen In Opening Game: Airtites To Play Refrigerators On Tuesday Night.," *Rhinelander Daily News*, 23 June 1928; "Rhinos Upset County Rivals In Return Go: Lefty Taylor And Mates Hold Hazelhurst Without A Run Until Eighth"; "Cold Breezes Fail To Check Rhino Attack," *Rhinelander Daily News*, 25 June 1928; "Russ Refuses To Call Game Despite Hour: Newsies Go Home In Dark With Score Standing 10-6 In Their Favor," *Rhinelander Daily News*, 28 August 1928; "Ripcos Tossed Out Of Wisconsin Valley League: Rapids Lands Local Berth: List Reasons," *Rhinelander Daily News*, 14 April 1933.

25. "Priests Will Scrap Rhinos: Clearwater Lake Team To Battle Local Nine On Fair Grounds Sunday."

26. "Ripco Ripples to Play Game In Minocqua: Rhinelander Ball Team Is Feature Of Island City's Fourth Program," *Rhinelander Daily News*, 2 July 1930; "Rotten Plays By Two Clubs Mar Interest: Two Rip Hurlers Fail To Show Stuff, And Fielders Play Like Ashland," *Rhinelander Daily News*, 7 July 1930; "Mike Stanke, Butch Manley Fail To Stick: Starting Hurlers Are Knocked From Box: Rhinelander Rally Dies," *Rhinelander Daily News*, 14 July 1930; "Rhinos Crack Prentice In Good Game," *Rhinelander Daily News*, 21 July 1930; "Ripcos Defeat Refrigerator Squad, 12 To 2."

27. "Ripcos Tossed Out Of Wisconsin Valley"; "Ripcos Will Enter Northern Lakes Loop: League Expected To Be Reorganized To Permit Rhinos' Entry," *Rhinelander Daily News*, 15 April 1933.

28. Joseph Miazga, correspondence/interview by author, Pensacola, Florida and Saint Paul, Minnesota, 15 February 2002.

29. Miazga correspondence/interview, 15 February 2002.

Chapter Four

John Kotz: Rhinelander Basketball Legend

The University of Wisconsin Badger men's basketball teams' return to the NCAA Final Four in 2000 rekindled interest in Wisconsin basketball. However, few people may realize that the peak of Badger basketball success was led by none other than a Rhinelander native. John Kotz was born in Rhinelander in 1919. Kotz's first introduction to basketball came in the church basketball league. He was a Roman Catholic, but his church had no basketball team. Consequently, he started attending the Baptist church where James Williams coached the basketball team. Kotz attended local schools growing up where his potential for success in basketball showed early. He attended Central Grade School where he helped lead Central to the fifth-grade championship. When he was a sixth grader, his class won the grade title and challenged the seventh graders to a game. They played only four-minute quarters then and after two periods with the score 19-0 in favor of Kotz's sixth graders, the seventh graders refused to continue. That sixth grade team then challenged the eighth grade team to a game that the sixth graders won by a smaller margin, 8 to 5. Kotz continued to excel in basketball and football as well before leaving the Rhinelander area in 1939 to begin a legendary college basketball career at University of Wisconsin-Madison.[1]

Kotz, a 6 foot 2 inch forward, played for the Badgers from the 1940-41 season to the1942-43 season. He was a star as a sophomore on the 1941 Badger basketball team that won the school's only NCAA basketball championship. In addition, he was named the outstanding player of the 1941 NCAA championship game. That 1940-41 team also established the longest winning streak in UW men's basketball history - 15 straight victories. Kotz added additional honors to the outstanding player designation including being named All Big Ten twice (1941 and

1942), All-American in 1942, the Big Ten MVP in 1942, and led the Big Ten in scoring in 1942. At the time he graduated from UW-Madison in 1942, he was the school's career scoring leader.[2]

Kotz's well-known college basketball career was preceded by a legendary career at Rhinelander High School. Kotz earned a larger-than-life reputation at R.H.S. Kotz helped lead the Hodags to three straight WIAA state basketball tournaments from 1937-1939 and led the Hodags to their only state basketball championship in 1939.[3] That team's accomplishments were remarkable and unequalled in Hodag basketball history. The starting five were Kotz, Bill Chariton, Penny Drivas, Ray Terzynski, and Ray Lenheiser.[4] Kotz, Lenheiser, and Drivas made first team all-conference in 1939 while Chariton and Terzynski made second-team all conference that year. In addition, at least three of the team members made first team All-State that year. According to Joe Bloom's *A Half-Century of Hodag Basketball: 1916-1969*, Kotz, Lenheiser, Drivas, and Terzynski were first-team All-state.[7] Bloom later changes his account in a July, 1982 *Our Town* article wherein he states that only Kotz, Lenheiser, and Drivas were first team All-State.[8] Nonetheless, using both accounts, it can be ascertained that Chariton was a second-team All-State selection that year and Terzynski either a first or second team All-State selection. This means that all five Hodag starters earned All-State honors that season. This is a remarkable achievement. Whether or not any other men's state high school basketball team has achieved such a feat is unknown. In addition to leading the Hodags to a state title in 1939, Kotz was named to All-Conference basketball teams during all four years that he played varsity basketball for the Rhinelander Hodags.[10]

It is worth noting here that Kotz, Lenheiser, and Drivas all played on the freshman team at UW-Madison the following season of 1939-40.[9] In those days, freshman could not play varsity basketball, but the freshman team defeated the varsity team in a memorable contest that included the three Rhinelander natives.[11]

While a member of the Hodag varsity squad during this period, Kotz also played a role in another part of state, if not national, basketball history. This was in the development of the one-handed push shot. The primary way of shooting a basketball in the 1930's was the two-handed shot. During the Hodag's 1937-39 visits to the state tournament in Madison, Kotz and the Hodag team introduced the one-handed shot or one-handed push shot to the rest of the state. The Hodags first introduced the shot to the state in 1937 in Madison just months after Stanford's Hank Luisetti popularized the shot by demonstrating better proficiency using the shot in New York's Madison Square Garden.[12]

The shot was considered revolutionary at that time and today Kotz is considered a pioneer in introducing the one-handed shot to the state.[13] Credit for the shot goes to Kotz's high-school basketball coach Russ Leksell. Leksell made every one of his players shoot that way. Leksell's theory was that each player has a dominant hand, and a two-handed shot could be thrown off target by the weaker hand and arm.[14] Joe Bloom notes Leksell's introduction of the shot in stating that Leksell was probably the first high-school coach to introduce the revolutionary tactics of one-handed shooting and a ball-control type of game. Prior to Leksell's coming to Rhinelander, all shots, except short shots, were taken with two hands, either overhead or underhanded.[15]

Despite the fact that Hodag basketball teams demonstrated outstanding success in utilization of the one-handed push shot for three years, it was still considered a unique way of shooting when Kotz came to UW-Madison. Bud Foster, the late UW coach who coached the Badgers to their 1941 NCAA title said that "Kotz was a one-handed shooter at Madison, which was something new at Wisconsin. That was before the jump shot. He would fake one way, two ways, three ways and get the shot off. He could really shoot."[16] Fritz Wegner, assistant coach of the 1941 team, remembers Kotz as "having a great one-handed shot, which was a novelty in those days. He had great hands and a head and fake that would send a guy right off the floor."[17] The one-handed shot is considered by many to be the precursor to the now commonly used jump shot seen in today's high school, college, and NBA games. The jump shot began to be used more often in the 1950's after being first used in the 1940's by college players such as Whitey Skoog and professional players including Joe Fulks, Paul Arizin, Jim Pollard, and Bob Pettit.[18] It is interesting to realize Rhinelander's connection to this part of basketball history through Russ Leksell and John Kotz.

While Kotz's collegiate and high-school performances are impressive, it is his off court character and life-long love of Rhinelander that many people most remember. After his college career, Kotz served four years in World War II with American amphibious forces in the Pacific theater. After his military discharge, he played professional basketball for a few seasons with the Sheboygan Redskins before beginning a career with Badger Sporting Goods in Madison. In noting Kotz's strong character, Fritz Wegner, the former UW assistant coach who recruited Kotz from Rhinelander, called Kotz an excellent person to coach who never had to have special treatment despite his popularity and ability. Instead, Kotz, the son of Polish immigrants, reflected his Depression-era upbringing with his strong work ethic. His work ethic helped him succeed on and off the court. As a college student in the days before athletic scholarships, he paid his room and board by sweeping the floors of the Capital Times newspaper. After starting his career with Badger Sporting Goods as a shipping clerk, he worked his way up to majority stockholder and president of the company. John Roach, who succeeded Kotz as president of Badger Sporting Goods, remarked that Kotz was often asked by high-school coaches to conduct impromptu shooting clinics as he traveled across the state selling sports equipment. Kotz always accepted the work, never wanting to disappoint these children. He loved helping out. During one of his speeches at a high-school banquet, Kotz told the audience about when he was a kid and he used to walk along the railroad tracks picking up coal that fell off the train to keep the family house warm. He grew up the hard way and remembered his tough times. Later in life, he golfed six days a week, until the spring of 1999. During his golf outings, he used to arrive at the Blackhawk Country Club in Madison every morning with a bag of doughnuts tucked under his arm. It didn't matter if it was summer, spring, fall or winter, he always fed the grounds crew with morning treats. Kotz was the type of person who would do anything for any of his friends, he just didn't want anybody to know about it.

Kotz's love for the Rhinelander area never wavered. His telephone answering machine told callers they had reached the home of the Hodag. He also proudly displayed "Hodag 2" on his license plates for many, many years until his death at the age of 80 in 1999.[19] Kotz was a Rhinelander legend who is likely to be remembered for a long, long time.

Courtesy of Rhinelander High School

WISCONSIN VALLEY CHAMPIONS — 1938
Seated: Chariton, Terzynski, Lenheiser, Kotz, Drivas, Lewis, Urquhart, Mgr. Mueller.
Standing: Coach Leksell, Mgr. George Stumpf, Morris, Poskie, Johnson, Parr, Makris, Danfield, Marks.

1938 Rhinelander Hodag Boys Basketball team. Wisconsin Valley Champions. John Kotz is seated 4th from the left.

SEASON'S RECORD — WON 20; LOST NONE

STATE TOURNAMENT SCORES				
	RHINELANDER	56	WAUWAUTOSA	21
	RHINELANDER	38	SHOREWOOD	21
	RHINELANDER	46	WAUSAU	29

Courtesy of Rhinelander High School

WISCONSIN STATE CHAMPIONS — 1939
Standing: Mgr. Dick Mueller, Bill Chariton, Ray Terzynski, John Kotz, Ray Lenheiser, Penny Drivas, Roy Lewis.
Kneeling: George Makris, Lodi Morris, Mascot Porky Counter (holding trophy), Dick Marks, Dale Danfield.

1939 Rhinelander Hodag Boys Basketball team. John Kotz is standing 4th from the left.

Courtesy of Rhinelander High School

Photos of the 1939 Rhinelander High School state championship boys basketball team.

Author's Collection

Thayer Street railroad tracks, where Kotz picked coal as a child. Rhinelander, WI.

Notes to Chapter Four

1. For a discussion of Kotz's childhood basketball memories see: Jack Cory, *Jack Cory's Scrapbook*, Northland Historical Society, Inc., Lake Tomahawk, Wis., 1985, 99.

2. For discussions of Kotz's collegiate basketball achievements see: Vic Feuerherd, "John Kotz: 1919-1999 Passing of a Legend; Kotz Led UW to '41 NCAA Title, Was a Pioneer of One-Handed Shot," *Wisconsin State Journal*, 11 May 1999, 1C; Rob Schultz, "Kotz A Legend on Court, And Friend to All Off It," *The Capital Times*, 11 May 1999, 1B; Bob Wolf, "Turning Back The Clock: Badgers' 59-year absence from Final Four Rekindles Memories of 1941 Squad," *Los Angeles Times*, 31 March 2000, D7; "Badgers' 1941 NCAA Title Run: Season to Remember: Championship Wasn't Expected", *The Capital Times*, 30 December 1997, 4B; "Special Sections – The Kohl Center: Thanks For The Memories: From Boxing to Buzzer Beaters," *Wisconsin State Journal*, 11 January 1998, 17; "Series: Sports in Wisconsin: The 20th Century," *Milwaukee Journal Sentinel*, 8 November 1999, 3; "John Kotz, former UW basketball player, dies at 80," *Associated Press Newswires*, 10 May 1999; "Kotz dies; led UW to NCAA title," *Milwaukee Journal Sentinel* 11 May 1999, 6; Rob Schultz and Joe Hart, "UW Basketball Star Kotz Dies at Age 80," *The Capital Times*, 10 May 1999, 1A; Gary D'Amato, "1941 Badgers Laid Bricks to Build Title," *Milwaukee Journal Sentinel*, 31 March 2000, 3S; Tom Butler, "Kotz Changed Basketball Forever in Wisconsin," *Wisconsin State Journal*, 11 May 1999, 1C; Tom Oates, "Kotz also A Giant Off The Court," *Wisconsin State Journal*, 12 May 1999, 1B.

3. Bultler, "Kotz Changed Basketball Forever in Wisconsin," 1C.

4. Joe Bloom, *Our Town*, July 1982.

5. Joe Bloom, *A Half Century of Hodag Basketball: 1916-1969* (Rhinelander, Wis. : by the author, 1969), 63.

6. Ibid., at 64.

7. Ibid., at 64.

8. Bloom, *Our Town*, July 1982.

9. Henry L. Miazga, interview by author, Rhinelander, Wis., 18 March 2001; Stanley Miazga, correspondence/interview by author, Pensacola, Fla. and Saint Paul, Minn., 23 February 2001.

10. Butler, "Kotz Changed Basketball Forever in Wisconsin," 1C; Bloom, *A Half Century of Hodag Basketball*, 105; "Badgers' 1941 NCAA Title Run: Season to Remember: Championship Wasn't Expected," 4B; Cory, *Jack Cory's Scrapbook*, 98.

11. Stanley Miazga, correspondence/interview by author, Pensacola, Fla. and Saint Paul, Minn., 23 February 2001.

12. For a discussion of Rhinelander's role in introducing the one-handed push shot to the state of Wisconsin see: Andy Baggot, "Field House Has Secrets, But No Lies: Grand Building Comes To End Of Duty As Tourney Host," *Wisconsin State Journal*, 13 March 1997, 1A; "Special Sections: The Kohl Center: Thanks For The Memories: From Boxing To Buzzer Beaters:," 17; Butler, "Kotz Changed Basketball Forever in Wisconsin," 1C; Bloom, *A Half Century of Hodag Basketball*, 19; Cliff Christl, "State Stars Escape From Wisconsin: The Cream Of Prep Crop Gets Away, History Says," *Milwaukee Journal*, 10 February 1991, C01. For a discussion of the one-handed push shot, its' development into the jump-shot, and Hank Luisetti's popularization of the shot see: Robert W. Peterson, *Cages To Jump Shots: Pro Basketball's Early Years* (New York, Oxford: Oxford University Press, 1990), 109, 110; John Christgau, *The Origins Of The Jump Shot: Eight Men Who Shook The World Of Basketball*, (Lincoln and London: University of Nebraska Press, 1999), 14, 15; William S. Jarrett, *Timetables of Sports History: Basketball*, (Facts on File, Inc., 1990), 20, 21, 25; *Jim Pollard Biography on NBA.com* website (as of June 24, 2002), http://global.nba.com/history/pollard_bio.html; "Basketball Hall of Honor To Induct Inaugural Class (10/31/01)" on *Pac-10 website* (as of March 1, 2002), www.pac-10.org/sports/m_baskbl/spec-rel/110201aaf.html.

13. Baggot, "Field House Has Secrets, But No Lies: Grand Building Comes To End of Duty As Tourney Host," 1A; Peterson, *Cages To Jump Shots*, 109, 110; Christgau, *The Origins Of The Jump Shot*, 14,15; Feuerherd, "John Kotz: 1919-1999: Passing Of A Legend: Kotz Led UW To '41 NCAA Title, Was A Pioneer Of One-Handed Shot," 1C.

14. Butler, "Kotz Changed Basketball Forever In Wisconsin," 1C.

15. Bloom, *A Half Century of Hodag Basketball*, 17.

16. Schultz and Hart, "UW Basketball Star Kotz Dies At Age 80," 1A.

17. Wolf, "Turning Back The Clock: Badgers' 59-Year Absence From Final Four Rekindles Memories of 1941 Squad", D7.

18. For a discussion of the jump-shot and Whitey Skoog's contribution to the development of it at the college level, see Christgau, *Origins Of The Jump Shot*, 26, 27. For a discussion of the jump shot's development at the professional level, see Peterson, *Cages To Jump Shots*, 44, 182; "Jim Pollard Biography" at *NBA.com*.

19. For a discussion of Kotz's off court character and remembrances of Kotz see: Oates, "John Kotz: 1919-1999: Passing Of A Legend: Kotz Led UW To '41 NCAA Title, Was A Pioneer Of One-Handed Shot," 1C; Cliff Christl, "State Stars Escape From Wisconsin: The Cream Of Prep Crop Gets Away,

History Says," *Milwaukee Journal*, 10 February 1991, C01; Associated Press, "Kotz Dies; Led UW To NCAA Title," 6; Michael Hunt, "Badgers Recall NCAA Cage Title: '41 Team Pulled Off Big Upset," *Milwaukee Sentinel*, 28 February 1991, 21; Lori Nickel, "Longtime Rivalry Remains The One That Teams, Fans Care About Most," *Milwaukee Journal Sentinel*, 23 December 1998, 1; Oates, "Kotz Also A Giant Off The Court," 1B; Doug Moe, "Boy Has Words To Remember Kotz," *The Capital Times*, 13 May 1999, 2A; "Badgers' 1941 NCAA Title Run: Season To Remember: Championship Wasn't Expected," 4B; Schultz, "Kotz A Legend On Court, And Friend To All Off It," 1B; Schultz and Hart, "UW Basketball Star Kotz Dies At Age 80," 1A; D'Amato, "1941 Badgers Laid Bricks To Build Title," 3S; Cory, *Jack Cory's Scrapbook*, 98, 99, 100; Butler, "Kotz Changed Basketball Forever In Wisconsin," 1C; Henry L. Miazga, interview by author, 18 March 2001, Stanley Miazga, interview/correspondence with author, 23 February 2001.

Chapter Five

Rhinelander's Hobo Jungle

While there is no hobo jungle in Rhinelander today and, indeed, very few across the country, hobo jungles were a common part of the American landscape during the Great Depression. Rhinelander, like so many other communities, was home to a hobo jungle during the 1920s and 1930s.

Hobo jungles were makeshift camps made up of shanties and tents that developed at nearly every major railroad junction in the country. People, primarily men, who rode railroad boxcars exited trains in search of a hobo jungle which was usually located near a stream so that travelers could wash up and make coffee. The jungles thrived in number primarily due to the Great Depression. In total, an estimated 4 million Americans rode railroad boxcars during the Great Depression.[1]

At the height of the Great Depression, over 300,000 individuals were riding these railroad boxcars, 250,000 of these being teenagers. Some of the teenagers left home because they felt they were a burden to their families; some fled homes shattered by unemployment and poverty. Fewer left because it seemed a great adventure. Either with the blessing of parents or as runaways, they left for the road and went in search of a better life. Many of these teenagers had looked for work in their hometown for two or three years. Unable to find stable work, they decided to hit the rails.[2]

The hobo jungle in Rhinelander existed in a wooded area east and north of the Rhinelander Paper Mill below the railroad trestle. The location is east of the Wisconsin River and then north to Phillips Street and south along the old Chicago and Northwestern Railroad tracks near Courtney Street.[3]

Most hoboes riding the railroad boxcars and living in the jungles primarily concerned themselves with finding their next meal. A common part of any hobo jungle during this time was the community pot. The pot consisted of whatever food the hoboes could come up with. Hoboes emptied their pockets in preparation for a stew cooked in the pot. One might have an onion, another might have potatoes and an ear of corn taken from a farmer's field. Often times, a hobo would walk into town and try to obtain work from a butcher or grocer in exchange for flour, sugar, cabbage, coffee or whatever might be needed for the pot. If he was lucky, he would find an hour or two's work to earn some food for the meal.[4]

Rhinelander's hobo jungle was no different. Stanley Miazga remembers the hobo jungle consisting of makeshift huts or shelters. The hoboes cooked soup in a gallon pail or other pots that were available. The soup consisted of whatever was available, a soup bone or meat donated by a friendly butcher and any assortment of vegetables the hoboes came up with. There was usually a fire going in the Rhinelander hobo jungle as well. Both Stanley Miazga and Eldore Huebner remember frequent fires or bonfires emanating from the hobo jungle. Huebner recalled a fire always brewing below the trestle when he walked over the trestle in the 1920s. Miazga remembers that the hoboes frequently had a bonfire to keep warm and likely also for boiling water as well.

An interesting type of work that some Rhinelander hoboes found to help sustain themselves was making baskets, flower boxes, and children's furniture. Lots of willow brush grew along the Wisconsin River below the Phillip Street dam and some hoboes would weave baskets from the flexible willow. Larger pieces of willow and birch were used to make the flower boxes and children's furniture. The hoboes would then sell their handiwork to earn money for food and other necessities.[5]

Another way hoboes across the country obtained food was to knock on the doors of homes and ask for a handout. Hoboes asked for a handout or a "lump" which was something typically received in a sack. Sometimes they enjoyed a "knee-shaker," eating a meal on a back porch, and occasionally a "sit-down," where they were invited inside the homes for a sit-down meal.[6] Rhinelander was no different in this regard. Ann Manning, Stanley Miazga, and Henry Miazga remember hoboes knocking on their door at their childhood home on Pelican Street. Their mother answered the door and prepared a nice, hot meal for the hoboes to eat on the porch.[7] According to Stanley, no one was ever admitted into the house. After the meal ended, there was a thank you and the man walked out to the Pelican Street sidewalk and headed down the street toward town.

Whether or not Rhinelander's hoboes had a system for finding homes where handouts were easily accessible is relatively unknown. Stories exchanged in hobo jungles often enabled the men to develop signs and symbols and establish a communication network that revealed which homes would receive them. The symbols also warned of homes they should stay away from. For example, a symbol resembling a plus sign informed hoboes that a home was a good place for a handout. A # symbol revealed that a police officer lived at the residence. Other symbols revealed where religious people lived, or people who would help them if they were sick. One symbol stood for a dishonest employer whom hoboes shouldn't work for. The location of these symbols varied. The symbols often were scrawled or scribbled on fence posts. Other symbols could be found scratched on train trestles. The symbols did not have to be written. Unwritten symbols included a single rock, numerous rocks, a single stick, and numerous sticks marking a home that contained a kindhearted person who would give food. Additional common symbols that were used at the time are printed below.[8]

Stanley Miazga believes that the hoboes in Rhinelander had some type of system or use of symbols as well, however unknown it was: "How these people could walk up the street right up to our house is a mystery to me…I still believe that our house had a marking known only to the hoboes."

The willingness to work in order to obtain their next meal was indicative of the way most hoboes lived their lives. Most hoboes were decent people trying to get by or trying to make some money for their families back home. Many hoboes maintained a certain level of respect and dignity. It was not uncommon for example for a community mirror to exist in a jungle. It was often a small mirror perched in a tree. The men used this mirror to shave. Despite the hoboes worthwhile goals of looking for employment and their generally good behavior, many southern towns in the United States drove young hoboes away without food and others subjected them to frontier-style justice. As young as sixteen, many were rounded up and sentenced to work on chain gangs or labor on the "pea farms," and other fields where corrupt law officials supplied the local growers with cost-free workers.[9]

Fortunately, Rhinelander was not like this. Long-time Rhinelander resident Eldore Huebner remembers growing up on Mason Street. He lived right next door to then Rhinelander Chief of Police Maurice Straub: "The Chief of Police left the hoboes alone. They didn't hurt anybody and we were unafraid of them. We considered them harmless."

Rhinelander's hobo jungle was also located near a popular children's hangout during the Great Depression, the "Hot Rocks." To understand the location of the "Hot Rocks," one must first understand the history of the physical area surrounding them. During the Great Depression, most of the employees of the Rhinelander Paper Mill walked to work. Many of those walking to work lived in an area known as the North Side of Rhinelander. These employees usually walked to the entrance of the Rhinelander Paper Mill located on Davenport Street to begin work. The Soo Line railroad crossed the Wisconsin River just south of the paper mill, but it was dangerous for the employees to walk across the railroad because of the heavy railroad traffic. To alleviate this problem, the paper mill built a wooden walk bridge across the Wisconsin River below the dam. This was known as the little green bridge. The bridge crossed the river to the land area between the main part of the river and the excavated canal. From here, a 10-15 foot wide walking bridge crossed the canal along the southeast wall of the paper mill allowing employees to continue walking from the North Side to the paper mill entrance on Davenport Street.[10]

The rocky area in the river north of the green bridge was known as the "Hot Rocks." Children from the near North and West Side parts of town played on the "Hot Rocks" frequently. Children would jump the rocks and play follow the leader. A deep pool existed in the "Hot Rocks" where Henry Miazga remembers learning to swim. Other children in these neighborhoods also learned to swim in this area near the jungle throughout the Great Depression. The hoboes lived in the jungle near the "Hot Rocks." They were well behaved and did not cause any trouble. Henry and Stanley Miazga each remember visiting the hobo jungle as children. Both remarked that the hoboes were well behaved and did not cause any trouble. According to Stanley, the hoboes willingly shared food with one another and did the best they could to sustain themselves. Henry remembered the hoboes with whom he interacted with in the jungle as being friendly and full of stories, many of which were tall tales. Some of the hoboes spoke only limited English as other languages were their primary language. Henry recalls speaking Polish with some of the hoboes for whom Polish was still their primary language. He also recalled many of the hoboes using nicknames in their travels instead of real names. This was a common part of the hobo culture in America at that time. He remembers men using the names Kaiser and Jingling Bullets in Rhinelander's hobo jungle.

The hobo jungle in Rhinelander eventually disappeared as did most hobo jungles across the United States. The Civilian Conservation Corps was developed in 1933 and lasted until 1942. This agency brought together over 2,000,000 people to work on projects across the United States. CCC members worked on numerous projects. The following is just a sample of the lasting work performed by the CCC's: building bridges, planting trees, running phone lines, draining swamps, restocking fish, building roads, trails, and fire lanes, creating state parks and campgrounds, and protecting banks from erosion. The Civilian Conservation Corps along with an improving economy and the advent of America's involvement in World War II took most men off of the railroad cars and out of the hobo jungles and into stable government, private, and military employment.[11]

Rhinelander's Hobo Jungle

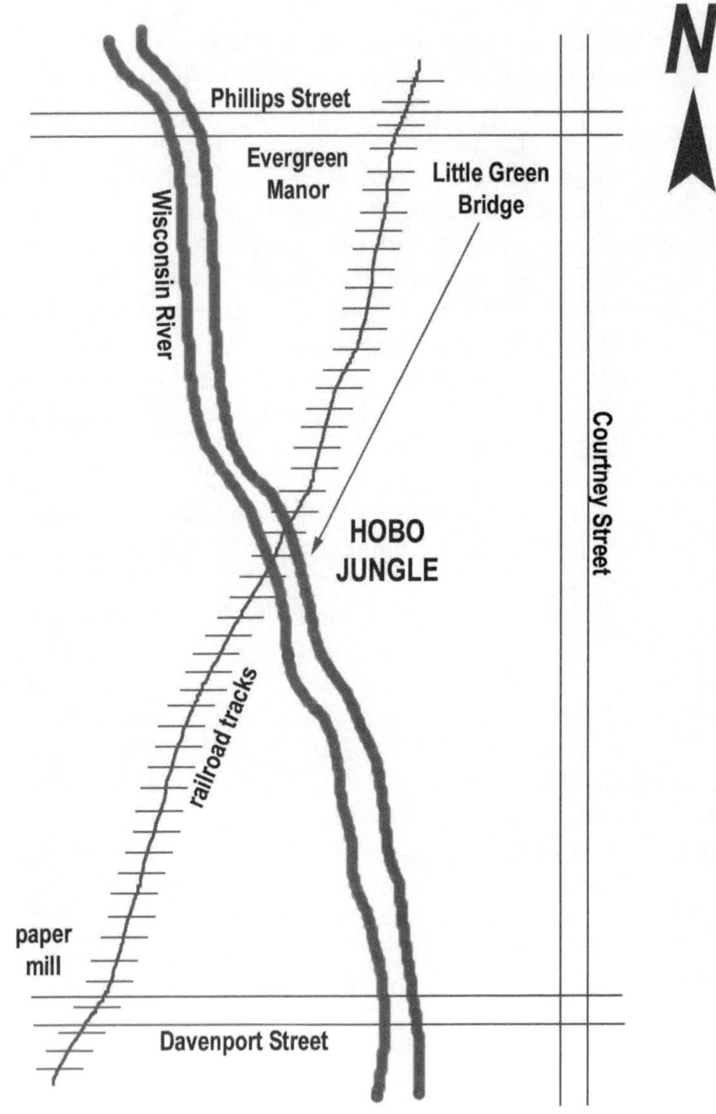

Used with permission, Library of Congress

Hobo making a meal in a Hobo Jungle.

Courtesy of the Rhinelander Public Library

Davenport St. Bridge and paper mill, ca. 1910. Rhinelander's Hobo Jungle was to the lower right of the postcard.

Author's collection

Davenport St. Bridge and paper mill, ca. 1922. Rhinelander's Hobo Jungle was to the lower right of the postcard.

Courtesy of the Rhinelander Public Library

Rhinelander Police Chief Maurice Straub. Straub was Chief of Police during most of the Great Depression Years.

Author's Collection

Little Green Bridge with site of the Hobo Jungle to the left. March 2001.

Author's Collection

Site of Rhinelander's depression-era hobo jungle. March 2001.

Used with permission, Minnesota Historical Society

Hobo camp or hobo jungle, ca. 1925.

Notes to Chapter Five

1. For a good discussion of the makeup and numbers of hobo jungles see D.J. Tice, "Saint Paul Man Recalls Life As A Hobo During The 1930s," *Associated Press Newswires*, 6 December 1999; Juanita Crawford Muiga, "Call Of The Rail: Wandering, Working Men Shaped Westsiders' Lives," *Tulsa World*, 24 May 2000, 1; Kevin Thomas, "Critic's Pick: 'Riding The Rails'," *Los Angeles Times*, 12 April 1998, 85; Richard Wormser, *Hoboes: Wandering In America, 1870-1940*, Walker and Company, New York, New York, 1994, 35, 39, 40-42, 48, 60, 79, 81, 111, 126; Duffy Littlejohn, *Hopping Freight Trains In America*, Sand River Press, Los Osos, Calif., 1993, 268-69; Charles Willeford, *I Was Looking For A Street*, The Countryman Press, Woodstock, Verm., 1988, 59.

2. For a good discussion of the phenomenon of riding railroad boxcars during the Great Depression see Errol Lincoln Uys, *Riding The Rails: Teenagers On The Move During The Great Depression*, TV Books, New York, New York, 1999, 2000, 11-44.

3. Eldore Huebner, interview by author, Rhinelander, Wis., 9 February 2001; Henry Miazga, interview by author, Rhinelander, Wis., 9 February 2001, 10 February 2001; Stanley Miazga, interview/correspondence with author, Pensacola, Fla. and Saint Paul, Minn., 23 February 2001.

4. Muiga, "Call Of The Rail: Wandering, Working Men Shaped Westsiders' Lives," 1; Tice, "Saint Paul Man Recalls Life As A Hobo During The 1930s,"; Uys, *Riding The Rails: Teenagers On The Move During The Great Depression*, 180-184.

5. Stanley Miazga interview/correspondence.

6. Uys, *Riding The Rails,* 145; Joanne Weintraub, "Hunger, Heartache Of Wanderers Found In Rumble, Smoke Of 'Rails'," *Milwaukee Journal Sentinel*, 12 April 1998, 2.

7. Henry Miazga interview; Stanley Miazga interview/correspondence; Ann Manning, interview/correspondence with author, Rhinelander, Wis. and Saint Paul, Minn., 29 January 2001.

8. Symbol table used with permission from Errol Uys, *Riding the Rails*, 167. For discussion of symbols or signs used by hoboes to communicate with one another see Uys, *Riding The Rails*, 166-168; "Steam Train" Maury Graham and Robert J. Hemming, *Tales Of The Iron Road: My Life As King Of The Hobos*, Paragon House, New York, New York, 1990, 95, 96; Pamela Li Calzi O'Connell, "'Hoppers' Find Forum On The 'Net," *Denver Post*, 28 September 1998, E09; Valryn Bush, "North Area: Town History Told In Memories," *Dayton Daily News*, 27 August 1998, Z68; Muiga, "Call Of The Rail: Wandering, Working Men Shaped Westsiders' Lives," 1.

[9] For hobo behavior see Muiga, "Call Of The Rail," 1; O'Connell, "'Hoppers' Find Forum On The 'Net," E09; Uys, *Riding The Rails*, 170, 183, 252. For discussion of the treatment of hoboes see Uys, *Riding The Rails*, 145; Wormser, *Hoboes: Wandering In America, 1870-1940*, 65, 83.

[10] Stanley Miazga interview; Henry Miazga interview.

[11] For a good discussion of the myriad duties performed by CCC members see George P. Reynolds, Susan Walker, Eliot Wigginton, and Rabun County High School Students, *Foxfire 10*, Anchor Books, New York, London, Toronto, Sydney, and Auckland, 1993, 240-41, 256-59; Uys, *Riding The Rails*, 40-44, 105, 199, 207, 216, 230-33, 244, 252-53, 259-61, 263-64; Anthony J. Badger, *The New Deal: The Depression Years, 1933-1940*, The Noonday Press, New York, New York, 1989, 170; William L. Katz, *An Album Of The Great Depression*, Franklin Watts Press, New York, London, 1978, 36, 41, 50; James F. Justin Civilian Conservation Corps Museum website (as of June 24, 2002), http://members.aol.com/famjustin/ccchis.html. For other discussion of the CCC's see Tice, "Saint Paul Man Recalls Life As A Hobo During The 1930s,"; Weintraub, "Hunger, Heartache Of Wanderers Found In Rumble, Smoke Of 'Rails'," 2; Michael J. Dunn, III, *Easy Going: Wisconsin's Northwoods: Vilas And Oneida Counties*, Tamarack Press, Madison, Wis., 1978, 28.

Chapter Six

Rhinelander Beer and the Rhinelander Brewery

Several aspects of the successful story of beer brewing in Wisconsin are unique to the state. Breweries' strong participation in Wisconsin community life is well established. They have played a major role in community life along side churches, schools, and mills. They have been steady employers. Breweries often purchased barley from local farmers and consumed huge quantities of ice cut from area lakes and millponds. Wisconsin breweries and local beer brands were abundant throughout Wisconsin in the 19th and 20th centuries. Northern and Northcentral Wisconsin was no different. In the 1940's alone, Rhinelander, Stevens Point, Wausau, Marshfield, Medford, Marathon, Merrill, and Shawano could all boast of having a local brewery. Local citizens were often as loyal to their local beer brand as they were to their local sports teams.[1]

Brewing in the Rhinelander area did not have an easy start. Town lots in the city of Rhinelander were first put up for sale on October 20, 1882. Each land deed contained a clause that stated: "Provided always that if said real estate shall be occupied at any time within five years from the date of this deed for the purposes of the sale of any spirituous or malt liquors without the consent of the family of the first part, when and in such case, the conveyance shall be void and the title shall revert and become invested in said party of the first part." This language barred the sale of any liquor on town lots sold in Rhinelander as of 1882. By 1891, Otto A. Hilgermann and Henry Danner were in Rhinelander perfecting plans for a brewery. Hilgermann, a Minneapolis, MN businessman, operated a furniture factory from 1887 through the early 1890s. The furniture factory included the manufacture of bar furnishings. Danner, a brewer with a well-known brewery in Jamestown, North Dakota, lost employment due to changes in the law.

In 1889 North Dakota was admitted to the Union with a clause prohibiting the sale or manufacture of any form of alcoholic beverage within its borders. After a year or so of litigation, the law was declared constitutional and Danner's brewery had to shut down. At this point, Danner teamed up with Hilgermann to build a brewery under the more friendly laws of Wisconsin.[2]

The duo incorporated the Rhinelander Brewing Company in 1891 and construction of the Rhinelander Brewing Company plant began late that same year under the supervision of Alex McRae. The chosen site was in Block 6 of the South Park addition to the City of Rhinelander bordering the Pelican River, today the Rhinelander Eye Clinic is located on the property. Construction was finished in April 1892 and the company's first product, named Rhinelander Beer, appeared on the market that month. The company then consisted of a 70 x 90-foot brewery heated by steam with an icehouse for cooling measuring approximately 30 x 85 feet. A large cellar with big vats stored 2,000 barrels of beer and a 60 x 62-foot refrigerator was placed on the premises holding 1,000 tons of ice. The brewery initially employed eight men and had an annual capacity of 10,000 to 15,000 barrels of beer. Danner's attempts to instill loyalty to his brewery among local citizens began almost as soon as the brewery began to produce beer, stating "the local brewery would keep the money that has been flowing into the coffers of the Milwaukee brewers at home."[3]

The partnership between Danner and Hilgermann did not last long. By September 1892 Hilgermann had purchased all of Danner's interest in the brewery and the partnership was dissolved. Hilgermann continued to run the brewery and in August 1893 the Rhinelander Brewing Company was re-organized to include John Hilber, James Keenan, and William Daniels as incorporators.[4]

Otto Hilgermann continued to be connected with and develop the Rhinelander brewery until his death in 1910. His attempts to market various brewery products such as Rhinelander Beer, "Our Beer," bock beer, "Budweiser" beer, Export Beer, and lager beer were evident in early advertisements such as the following:[5]

Don't Let Beer Get The Best Of You!

—Get the Best of BEER Which is—

Rhinelander Beer!

Rhinelander Brewing Co.

BOTTLED BEER.

Our bottling works is now in full operation and we are now able to supply private families with first-class beer by the case in either pint or quart bottles.

Why Not Patronize the Home Brewery?

Rhinelander Brewing Co.

HERE'S WHAT MAKES YOU WANT YOUR DINNER

A glass of Rhinelander beer is just about the finest thing to create an appetite for a worth-while meal you ever struck—beats any cocktail concocted Doesn't go to the head, does prepare the stomach for more solid nourishment. We guarantee its purity—you will swear by it as to its taste and its appetite provoking quality. Yet is costs only $1 per case of 18 pints delivered to your home.

TRY OUR MALT TONIC
IT BUILDS YOU UP

RHINELANDER BREWING CO.

Better'n Red Lemonade, B'gosh,

for a Fourth of July bracer is our bracing and wholesome Lager Beer. What is more nourishing and invigorating on a hot, sultry day than a drink of cold, sparkling and refreshing beer. If you have not tested it you will find pleasure in doing so when you are fagged out from the heat. Try it.

Rhinelander Brewing Co

THE BEST PROOF OF ITS PURITY

lies in the fact that physicians prescribe pure beer for their patients. Its qualities as a tonic and general rejuvenator of the human system are recognized by all familiar with its merits. Its freedom from adulterants, the patience, skill and care exercised in its manufacture, recommend it to you. Sold in bottles at $1.00 per 18 pints or 12 quarts, delivered at your door.

RHINELANDER BREWING COMPANY.

Concern over impurities in beer products were common during this period of brewing. The Rhinelander Brewing Company made sure the public was aware of the high quality of its brewery products. An August 6, 1892 article/advertisement in the *New North* states that "fifty dollars reward will be paid by the management of the Rhinelander Brewery to any person that will submit evidence that their beer contains any drugs or impurities. It is made of malt and hops and is perfectly pure and healthy. You should call for "Rhinelander" and thereby insure yourself against beers containing deleterious matter."

The brewery also made sure the public was aware of its' founding brewmaster's background. An April 30, 1892 article in the *New North* informs the reader that Henry Danner was an experienced brewer of 25 years and that his vast knowledge and acquaintance of brewing beer guarantees the finest product.

Hilgermann's role in the Rhinelander Brewing Company waned over the years, but he remained a steadfast promoter of, and contributor to, the city of Rhinelander. Hilgermann established Hilgermann Park, which opened to the public in June 1899. Hilgermann Park was located on the opposite side of the Pelican River from the brewery. A bridge was built across the river and a road along the riverbank a short distance down the river was constructed. This road led to a pavilion and refreshment stands for the public's enjoyment. Hilgermann Park became a hotbed of social activity including dances and concerts until at least 1910. It is unclear when Hilgermann Park ceased to exist. Hilgermann's contributions to Rhinelander also included helping start other businesses in Rhinelander such as the Rhinelander Refrigerator Company and Rhinelander Telephone Company. In addition, he made numerous real estate investments in the city of Rhinelander.[6]

The making of Rhinelander Beer and other Rhinelander Brewing Company products required the use of large quantities of ice. Ice was an important commodity in the early days of brewing. Ice was already used in home iceboxes and companies delivered ice to these homes. The development of breweries in Wisconsin in the late 1800s created yet another market for ice companies. Beers such as lager beer required cool temperatures for both storage and fermentation. Wisconsin's cold weather and abundance of lakes provided an ample supply of ice. So great was the demand for ice in the late 1800s that breweries to the south of the state often bought Wisconsin ice and had it shipped to them by expensive rail.[7]

The Rhinelander Brewing Company obtained their ice from the

Pelican River near their plant. After a fire destroyed much of the plant in November, 1897 a new building was built of solid brick from the basement up and a new ice house constructed as well. The Pelican River continued to be the main source of brewery ice into the early 1900s as the Brewery would send a crew of men and teams horses onto the river to dig out sufficient ice to fill the ice house at the brewery.[8]

Additional icehouses existed in the Rhinelander area in the early part of the century on River Street, which took ice from the Wisconsin River, Alban Street, which took ice from Boom Lake, and Pine Lake which took ice from Lake Creek. It is unclear whether these icehouses supplied the brewery with any of its' ice. The process of ice harvesting was tedious. Ice harvesting took two to three weeks. First a team (later, a tractor) scraped the snow off the ice as soon as it was 10 to 12 inches thick. The ice would then be cut by man-operated saws which were later replaced by gasoline powered saws. Teams of horses then pulled the ice chunks out and hoisted them onto wagon sleds that hauled several ice cakes to a load.

Perhaps the largest icehouse in the Rhinelander area was the Rhinelander Ice and Fuel Company. Rhinelander Ice and Fuel handled 3,000 tons of ice a year, putting it up each winter in Boom Lake. Despite its' numerous years of activity, Rhinelander Ice and Fuel never had a bad accident. Warning signals were erected on Boom Lake to mark the corners of the ice-gathering field to keep skaters away. Much of the ice from Rhinelander Ice went into refrigerators that were made in Rhinelander. The Rhinelander Refrigerator Company, of which Otto Hilgermann was part-owner used the ice in manufacturing its' Airtites and Chieftains refrigerators. Rhinelander Ice and Fuel also built commercial coolers. The ice was packed in sawdust, readily available from the several sawmills in the area, and well kept until summer.[9]

Icehouses helped make the Rhinelander Brewing Company successful well into the early 1900s. This success lasted until Prohibition found its' way from Danner's North Dakota of 1899 to Hilgermann's Wisconsin of 1919. On August 17, 1917, the United States Senate passed the prohibition resolution. On December 17, 1917, the House of Representatives did the same. Section one of the resolution read: "After one year from the ratification of this article the manufacture, sale, or transportation of intoxicating liquors within, the importation thereof into, or the exportation thereof from the United States and all territories subject to the jurisdiction thereof for beverage purposes is hereby prohibited." Thirty-six states ratified the amendment on January 29, 1919 and prohibition, also known as the 18th amendment to the U.S. Constitution, became the law of the land on January 16, 1920.[10]

The roots of the federal prohibition of alcohol movement could be seen at the time of Danner's decision to leave North Dakota and move to Wisconsin in 1889. The prohibition movement continued state by state through 1919. By 1919, thirty-two states had adopted prohibition either as part of their constitutions or as part of their state statutes. Wisconsin was one of sixteen states that did not have statewide prohibition of alcohol before passage of the 18th Amendment.[11] The Rhinelander Brewing Company closed and shipped its equipment to Mexico shortly after Prohibition began. Most old-time saloonkeepers quit the business and a new crop of soft drink parlors sprang up.[12]

The next 13 years saw a battle on the national front between advocates for strict enforcement of the 18th Amendment and advocates for repeal of Prohibition. Sentiment in Rhinelander may have reflected statewide sentiment. Many in the state did not greet the passage of the 18th Amendment with great enthusiasm.[13] Numerous people lost employment. Brewing had been Wisconsin's fifth-largest industry and Wisconsin agriculture saw an important cash crop in malting barley virtually disappear. In addition, many saw prohibition as an unwarranted invasion of their privacy rights.[14] On the other side were the advocates who claimed that prohibition had its merits. At a congregational church service in Rhinelander in June 1922 the pastor Reverend Charles H. Wicks told of the law-enforcement convention at Milwaukee he attended along with several other Rhinelander citizens. Mr. Wicks claimed that the convention boasted of the successes of prohibition, specifically a 60% reduction in drunkenness and a reduction in poverty.[15]

Whatever the merits of either side's argument, the Democratic party at its national convention in 1932 adopted a plank that favored the repeal of the 18th Amendment and an immediate modification so that beer would be declared legal for manufacture and sale. In November 1932, democrat Franklin D. Roosevelt was elected President and a democratic party majority was elected to Congress. The democrats acted swiftly enacting the Cullen-Harrison Bill in March 1933 legalizing 3.2 percent alcohol by volume beer.[16] Rhinelander residents greeted the news heartily and happily. Local citizens unanimously declared that the 3.2 percent beer was an excellent beer. Citizens also declared that this new beer contained much less alcohol than the wildcat and spiked beer that was illegally sold in the Rhinelander area during prohibition. In addition, people thought that it had a better taste, went down more smoothly, and didn't have any gas-like after effects. The first 3.2 percent beer arriving in Rhinelander during this time came primarily from Manitowoc, Minneapolis, and Stevens Point.[17]

The return of beer to Rhinelander also brought about a boost in local business. Local beer distributors gave at least 13 unemployed people work. In addition, some new bars were opened, existing businesses had to hire new help, and restaurants needed additional wait-staff.[18] By December 5, 1933, thirty-six states had ratified the 21st Amendment to the U.S. Constitution that repealed the 18th Amendment and officially ended prohibition. By December 23, 1933 the Rhinelander Brewing Company was back in business and ready to distribute its new 4.5 percent beer.[19]

After the repeal of prohibition, Rhinelander Brewing Company continued to be successful. The brewery's labels grew to include Rhinelander, Rhinelander Export, Shorty Export, and Shorty.[20] Perhaps the best known of these labels was the Shorty. Early in January 1940 the brewing company began advertising Shorty's in the local newspaper. The name "Shorty" was the idea of then Rhinelander Brewing Company president Larry Henning and Walter Yankee. It was advertised as the first baby of the new year for the family of Rhinelander Export. "Shorty," a seven-ounce bottle of beer, gained immediate popularity with the public. At the time there were only a couple of other breweries producing seven-ounce bottles of beer across the country, but none in Wisconsin. "Shorty" cartoons were featured in advertisements and calendars. Every local bar displayed "Shorty" bottles with wooden arrows speared through the middle. Other "Shorty" bottles included shaker caps to serve as salt and pepper dispensers. When "Shorty" first appeared it sold for a dime.[21]

Rhinelander Export was another popular Rhinelander Brewing Company product both before and after World War II. Additional successful products of the Rhinelander Brewing Company included canned beer introduced in 1969, a 64-ounce bottle known variously as a picnic or willie, and kegs of one-eighth, one-quarter, and one-half barrel size that were delivered to taverns throughout the region.[22] The popularity of the company's products likely helped convince brewery management to embark on a major modernization program in 1960. A new brew kettle, mash tun, hops separator, and grits cooker were installed. These were the first major improvements in the brewery since

1948. In 1960 the brewery had a forty thousand-barrel capacity. In a single day it could fill seventy-six thousand bottles of seven-ounce shorties, fifty-eight thousand cans, and forty-eight thousand bottles of Export. The brewery used forty-six distributors in Wisconsin, Minnesota, northern Michigan, and Chicago to help sell its' products and owned warehouses in Rhinelander, Wausau, and Omro.[23]

Post-war success of the company seemed evident when they had the best single-month sales in its history in July 1959.[24] However, after years and years of being a major employer in the Rhinelander area, the Rhinelander Brewing Company employed only 26 people by June 1967. During that month, the company was placed into receivership after bankruptcy proceedings. Competition from Milwaukee and increased costs of production proved to be too difficult for the Rhinelander Brewing Company to overcome. The dumping of 291 barrels of beer from the vats on the morning of June 30, 1967 marked the closing of the plant and company. The final bottle to come off the bottling line was given to Mrs. Lilllian Lassig, general manager and vice-president of the firm. The Joseph Huber Brewing Company of Monroe, Wisconsin purchased the Rhinelander label and beer recipes after the brewery closed in 1967.[25] The Huber Brewing Company continues to brew Rhinelander Beer and Rhinelander Bock beer today.[26]

HILGERMAN PARK

NOW OPEN.

Visitors Welcome.

Admission Free.

Music Every Sunday, Afternoon and Evening. Perfect Order Maintained.
Dance Floor 32x76 feet.

KRANTZ & BOLLMAN, Proprietors.

Dance Tickets 25 Cents.

Early advertisement for Hilgerman Park. *Rhinelander Herald*, July 14, 1900.

Courtesy of the Rhinelander Public Library

Otto Hilgermann, Rhinelander Brewery founder.

Courtesy of the Rhinelander Public Library

Rhinelander Brewing Company in the 1890s.

Courtesy of the Rhinelander Public Library

Rhinelander Brewing Company truck from the 1930s.

Courtesy of the Rhinelander Public Library

Rhinelander Brewing Company truck from the late 1930s—early 1940s.

Courtesy of the Rhinelander Public Library

Rhinelander Brewing Company truck from the 1950s.

Courtesy of the Rhinelander Public Library

Rhinelander Brewing Company truck from the 1960s.

Author's collection

Rhinelander Export beer label from the 1960s.

Author's collection

Rhinelander Super Export beer label from the 1960s.

Author's collection

Rhinelander Export beer label from the 1950s-1960s.

Author's collection

Rhinelander Super Export beer label from the 1950s-1960s.

Notes to Chapter Six

1. For a discussion of Wisconsin's rich brewing tradition see Jerry Apps, *Breweries Of Wisconsin*, The University Of Wisconsin Press, Madison, Wis., 1992, xx, 223-29.

2. For a description of early town lots in Rhinelander see T.V. Olsen, *Birth Of A City, The Rhinelander Country: Volume Two*, Pineview Publishing, Rhinelander, Wis., 1983, 105, 108. For a discussion of Hilgermann and Danner's early days in Rhinelander see *The New North*, 10 September 1891, 1; *The New North, 5 November 1891, 1; The New North*, 30 April 1892, 1; *The New North*, 16 September 1891, 2.

3. For discussion of the construction of the early brewery see *New North*, 10 September 1891, 1; *New North*, 30 April 1892.

4. *The New North*, 17 September 1892, 1,2; *The New North*, 24 September 1892, 1.

5. References to these brewery products and/or the advertisements themselves can be found at *The New North*, 21 May 1892; *The New North*, 27 August 1892; *The New North*, 11 May 1895; *The Rhinelander Herald*, 30 June 1900; *The New North*, 30 November 1899, 3; *The Rhinelander Herald*, 24 September 1898, 4; *The New North*, 9 April 1908, 4; *The Rhinelander Herald*, 15 June 1907, 3; *The Rhinelander Herald*, February 1901, 2.

6. For a discussion of Hilgermann's contributions to the city of Rhinelander see *The New North*, 14 December 1893; *The New North*, 17 June 1899; *The New North, 1 July* 1899; "Dance At Hilgermann Park," *The New North*, 22 July 1899; *The New North*, 6 September 1902; "Eagles Picnic At Hilgermann Park," *The New North*, 27 June 1908; *The New North*, 2 May 1927 (concerning Hilgermann's death); *The New North*, 5 May 1927 (Hilgermann's Obituary); Jones, *History Of Lincoln, Oneida And Vilas Counties*, 1924; T.V. Olsen, *Our First Hundred Years: A History Of Rhinelander*, 1981, 70; T.V. Olsen, et al, *Oneida County: 1887-1987: Centennial History Edition* (Rhinelander, Wis., 1987), 51.

7. Apps, *Breweries Of Wisconsin*, 19, 20, 52.

8. As to obtaining ice from the Pelican River see *The New North*, 11 February 1892; *The New North*, 17 February 1900. As to construction of the new plant after fire destroyed the first plant see *The New North* 6 November 1897.

9. For an excellent discussion of Rhinelander's icehouses see Jack Cory, "Firm Once Active In Coal And Ice Trade Now Closes Doors As Demand Dwindles," *Rhinelander Daily News*, 26 January 1971.

10. Apps, *Breweries Of Wisconsin*, 67.

[11.] Ibid. at 66.

[12.] "Liquor Reintroduced To Northwoods After Prohibition," *Rhinelander Daily News*, 5 December 2001, 1.

[13.] Robert Gough, *Farming The Cutover: A Social History Of Northern Wisconsin, 1900-1940*, University Press Of Kansas, Lawrence, Kan., 1997, 152; Apps, *Breweries Of Wisconsin*, 72.

[14.] Ibid. at 72.

[15.] "Shall We Retain Prohibition Law?," *The New North*, 1922 June.

[16.] Apps, *Breweries Of Wisconsin*, 73.

[17.] For discussion of Rhinelander's reaction to the introduction of 3.2 percent beer see "Rhinos Learn Beer Is Boost For Business: More Men Have Jobs; Even Bakeries Get Benefit From Brew's Return," *Rhinelander Daily News*, 10 April 1933, 1; "Beer Is Good, Verdict Here After Trials: Old Taste Is There, Say Testers; Trucks Battle Snow, Mud And Police," *Rhinelander Daily News*, 7 April 1933, 1; "Breweries Of State Center In Rush Today: Manufacturers Move To Put Legal Beverage On Sale Promptly," "19 States Will Have 3.2 Beer By Tomorrow," "No State Law On Regulation Of Beer Sales: Substitute Plan Not To Be Acted Upon Before Friday," *Rhinelander Daily News*, 6 April 1933, 1.

[18.] "Rhinos Learn Beer Is Boost For Business," 1.

[19.] "Liquor Reintroduced To Northwoods After Prohibition," 1.

[20.] Apps, *Breweries Of Wisconsin*, 205.

[21.] Kris Gilbertson, "'Shorty's' Birth Created A Stir In Rhinelander," *Rhinelander Daily News*, 16 January 1990, 1.

[22.] Ibid. at 1; Kris Gilbertson, "Dietz Saw Rhinelander Beer Through Many Transitions," *Rhinelander Daily News*, 1984.

[23.] Apps, *Breweries Of Wisconsin*, 204, 205.

[24.] Ibid. at 205.

[25.] For a discussion of competition from Milwaukee brewers and increased costs of production helping to bring an end to the Rhinelander Brewing Company and the sale of the label to the Joseph Huber Brewing Company see Apps, *Breweries Of Wisconsin*, 204, 205. For a discussion of the final days of the Rhinelander Brewing Company see "Brewing Firm's Creditors Will Meet In Wausau," *Rhinelander Daily News*, 8 June 1967, 2; "Decision On Brewing Firm's Future Thursday," *Rhinelander Daily News*, 20 June 1967, 2; "Brewing Firm In Receivership After Hearing," *Rhinelander Daily News*, 23 June 1967, 1, 2; "Brewery Ceases Operations Today," *Rhinelander Daily News*, 30 June

1967, 1, 2; "Brewing Firm Creditors Get Aug. 3 Deadline," *Rhinelander Daily News*, 21 July 1967, 2; "Hearing Aug. 17 May Say Brewing Firm Bankrupt," *Rhinelander Daily News*, 8 August 1967, 2.

[26.] For references to today's Rhinelander Beer and Rhinelander Bock Beer see the website www.berghoffbeer.com/history.htm (as of June 24, 2002).

Bibliography

Books

Apps, Jerry, *Breweries of Wisconsin*. The University of Wisconsin Press, Madison, Wis., 1992.

Badger, Anthony J., *The New Deal: The Depression Years, 1933-1940*. The Noonday Press, New York, N.Y., 1989.

Bloom, Joseph, *A Half Century of Hodag Basketball: 1916-1969*. By the author, 1969.

Chadwick, Bruce, *Baseball's Hometown Teams: The Story of The Minor Leagues*. Abbeville Press Publishers, New York, London, and Paris, 1994.

Christgau, John, *The Origins Of The Jump Shot: Eight men Who Shook The World of Basketball*. Lincoln and London: University of Nebraska Press, 1999.

Cory, Jack. *Jack Cory's Scrapbook*. Northland Historical Society Press, Lake Tomahawk, Wis., 1985.

Dunn, Michael III, *Easy Going: Wisconsin's Northwoods: Vilas and Oneida Counties*. Tamarack Press, Madison, Wis., 1978.

Gard, Robert E., *This Is Wisconsin*. Wisconsin House, Spring Green, Wis., 1969.

Girardin, G. Russell and Helmer, William J., *Dillinger: The Untold Story*. Indiana University Press, 1994.

Graham, "Steam Train" Maury and Hemming, Robert J., *Tales of The Iron Road: My Life As King of The Hobos*. Paragon House, New York, N.Y., 1990.

Gough, Robert, *Farming The Cutover: A Social History of Northern Wisconsin, 1900-1940*. University Press of Kansas, Lawrence, Kans., 1997.

Hollatz, Tom, *Gangster Holidays: The Lore and Legends Of The Bad Guys*. North Star Press of Saint Cloud, Inc., Saint Cloud, Minn., 1996.

Jarrett, William S., *Timetables of Sports History: Basketball*. Facts on File, Inc., 1990.

Jones, George O., Mcvean, Norman s., et al. *History of Lincoln, Oneida, and Vilas Counties*. H.C. Cooper, JR. Co., Minneapolis and Winona, MN, 1924.

Katz, William L., *An Album Of The Great Depression*. Franklin Watts Press, New York, London, 1978.

Kortenhof, Kurt D., *Long Live The Hodag: The Life And Legacy Of Eugene Simeon Shepard: 1854-1923*. Hodag Press, Rhinelander, Wis., 1996.

Littlejohn, Duffy, *Hopping Freight Trains In America*. Sand River Press, Los Osos, Calif., 1993.

Maccabee, Paul, *John Dillinger Slept Here: A Crooks' Tour of Crime and Corruption in Saint Paul, 1920-1936*. Minnesota Historical Society Press, Saint Paul, Minn., 1995.

Olsen, T.V., *Birth of a City, The Rhinelander Country: Volume Two*. Pineview Publishing, Rhinelander, Wis., 1983.

Olsen, T.V., et al., *Oneida County: 1887-1987: Centennial History Edition*. Rhinelander, Wis., 1987.

Olsen, T.V., *Our First Hundred Years: A History Of Rhinelander*. Rhinelander, Wis., 1981. Also published as *Our First Hundred Years: The Rhinelander Country, Volume Three*. Pineview Publishing, Rhinelander, Wis., 1983.

Peterson, Robert W., *Cages To Jump Shots: Pro Basketball's Early Years*. Oxford University Press, New York, Oxford, 1990.

Reynolds, George P., Walker, Susan, Wigginton, Eliot, and Rabun County High School Students, *Foxfire 10*. Anchor Books, New York, London, Toronto, Sydney, and Auckland, 1993.

Thornley, Stew, *On To Nicollet: The Glory And Fame Of The Minneapolis Millers*. Nodin Press, Minneapolis, Minn., 2000.

Toland, John, *The Dillinger Days*, Da Capo Press, New York, N.Y., 1995.

Uys, Errol Lincoln, *Riding The Rails: Teenagers On The Move During The Great Depression*. TV Books, New York, N.Y., 1999, 2000.

Willeford, Charles, *I Was Looking For A Street*. The Countryman Press, Woodstock, VT., 1988.

Wormser, Richard, *Hoboes: Wandering In America, 1870-1940*. Walker And Company, New York, N.Y., 1994.

Interviews

Huebner, Eldore, longtime Rhinelander resident. Interviewed by author. February 9, 2001.

Manning, Ann, longtime Rhinelander resident. Correspondence with author. January 29, 2001.

Miazga, Henry, longtime Rhinelander resident. Interviewed by author. February 9, 2001, February 10, 2001, March 18, 2001, and June 16, 2001.

Miazga, Joseph, longtime Rhinelander resident. Correspondence with author. February 15, 2002.

Miazga, Stanley, longtime Rhinelander resident. Interviewed by author. August, 2001. Correspondence with author. February 23, 2001.

Newspapers

Associated Press Newswires. May 10, 1999 and December 6, 1999.

Chicago Tribune. Chicago, Ill. Daily. March 13, 1994.

Cory, Jack.. Newspaper Clipping Collection. Rhinelander Historical Society, Rhinelander, Wis.

Dayton Daily News. Dayton, Ohio. Daily. August 27, 1998.

Denver Post. Denver, Col. Daily. September 28, 1998.

Indianapolis Star. Indianapolis, Ind. Daily. July 24, 1994.

Lakeland Times. Minocqua, Wis. Bi-weekly. February 9, 2001.

Los Angeles Times. Los Angeles, Calif. Daily. April 12, 1998 and March 31, 2000.

Madison Capital Times. Madison, Wis. Daily. Selected Issues: December 30, 1997 through May 13, 1999.

Milwaukee Journal. Milwaukee, Wis. Daily. February 10, 1991.

Milwaukee Journal Sentinel. Milwaukee, Wis. Daily. Selected Issues: April 12, 1998 through March 31, 2000.

Milwaukee Sentinel. Milwaukee, Wis. Daily. February 28, 1991.

New North. Rhinelander, Wis. Weekly. Selected Issues: September, 1891 through April, 1934.

Orlando Sentinel. Orlando, Fla. Daily. November 28, 1992.

Our Town. Rhinelander, Wis. Weekly. Selected Issues: May 29, 1977 through July, 1982.

Rhinelander Daily News. Rhinelander, Wis. Daily. Selected Issues: July 1920 through December 2001.

Rhinelander Herald. Rhinelander, Wis. Weekly. Selected Issues: September 24, 1898 through June 15, 1907.

Tulsa World. Tulsa, Okla. Daily. May 24, 2000.

Wisconsin State Journal. Madison, Wis. Daily. Selected Issues: March 13, 1997 through May 12, 1999.

On-line Resources

Bardsley, Marilyn and May, Allan, John Dillinger: Little Bohemia: The Crime Library: Feature Stories, *www.crimelibrary.com/americana/dillinger/dillingermain.htm.* Current as of September 21, 2002.

Berghoff Beer Website, *www.berghoffbeer.com/history.htm.* Current as of September 21, 2002.

Federal Bureau Of Investigation Website, John Dillinger: Famous Cases, *www.fbi.gov/libref/historic/famcases/dillinger/dillinger.htm.* Current as of September 21, 2002.

Justin, James F. Civilian Conservation Corps Museum Website, h*ttp://members.aol.com/famjustin/ccchis.html.* Current as of September 21, 2002.

NBA.com Website, Jim Pollard Biography, *http://global.nba.com/history/pollard_bio.html.* Current as of September 21, 2002.

Pac-10 Website, Basketball Hall Of Honor To Induct Inaugural Class (10/31/01), *www.pac-10.org/sports/m_baskbl/spec-rel/110201aaf.html.* Current as of March 1, 2002.

Program Transcript, "George Wallace: Settin' The Woods On Fire," *The American Experience.* Also available at *www.pbs.org* as of September 21, 2002.

About the Author

Mark Miazga was born and raised in Rhinelander, Wisconsin. He graduated from Rhinelander High School in 1987, the University of Wisconsin at Eau Claire in 1991, and Hamline University School of Law in 1996. He currently works and resides in Saint Paul, Minnesota.

The author enjoying a Rhinelander Beer, October 2002.

Order Information

Questions, comments or inquiries for additional copies of **Tales of the Northwoods** should be directed to the author at:

Mark Miazga
1237 Jessie Street
Saint Paul, MN 55101

About Hodag Press

Hodag Press was established in 1993 to produce and distribute publications with a local or regional appeal. In addition to ***Tales of the Northwoods***, Hodag Press has published two previous titles: ***Sugar Camp 1891-1941*** and ***Long Live the Hodag!*** Both full-length books are still in print and available directly from Hodag Press (see below for pricing and complete bibliographical citations).

Kortenhof, Kurt Daniel. ***Long Live the Hodag! The Life and Legacy of Eugene Simeon Shepard: 1854-1923.*** Rhinelander, WI: Hodag Press, 1996. 160 pages. ISBN: 0-9653745-0-5.
(hardcover \$32; soft cover \$12)

Kortenhof, Kurt Daniel. ***Sugar Camp 1891-1941: The Origin and Early History of a Northern Wisconsin Community.*** Rhinelander, WI: Hodag Press, 1993. 97 pages. ISBN: 0-9653745-1-3.
(hardcover \$30; soft cover \$10)

Hodag Press also offers consulting, publishing and distribution services to those interested in transforming a manuscript into a professional publication.

To order Hodag Press titles or to discuss contracting with Hodag Press to publish a manuscript, please direct correspondence to the address below.

Hodag Press®
131st Street West
Savage, MN 55378

hodagpress@msn.com